Andre

Everard Van Braam Houckgeest

An Authentic Account of the Embassy of the Dutch East-India Company,

to the court of the emperor of China, in the years 1794 and 1795: subsequent to that of the Earl of Macartney. Vol. 2

Andre

Everard Van Braam Houckgeest

An Authentic Account of the Embassy of the Dutch East-India Company,
to the court of the emperor of China, in the years 1794 and 1795: subsequent to that of the Earl of Macartney. Vol. 2

ISBN/EAN: 9783337245184

Printed in Europe, USA, Canada, Australia, Japan

Cover: Foto ©ninafisch / pixelio.de

More available books at **www.hansebooks.com**

AN
AUTHENTIC ACCOUNT
OF THE
EMBASSY
OF THE
DUTCH EAST-INDIA COMPANY,
TO THE
COURT OF THE EMPEROR OF CHINA,
In the Years 1794 and 1795;
(SUBSEQUENT TO THAT OF THE EARL OF MACARTNEY.)
CONTAINING A DESCRIPTION OF
SEVERAL PARTS OF THE CHINESE EMPIRE,
UNKNOWN TO
EUROPEANS;
TAKEN FROM THE JOURNAL OF
ANDRÉ EVERARD VAN BRAAM,
MANY YEARS CHIEF OF THE DIRECTION OF THAT
COMPANY, AND SECOND IN THE EMBASSY.
TRANSLATED FROM THE ORIGINAL OF
M. L. E. MOREAU DE SAINT-MERY.

With a correct Chart of the Route.

VOL. II.

LONDON:
PRINTED FOR R. PHILLIPS, NO. 71, ST. PAUL'S CHURCH-
YARD, AND SOLD BY J. DEBRETT, PICCADILLY; LEE
AND HURST, PATERNOSTER-ROW; AND BY
ALL OTHER BOOKSELLERS.

1798.

JOURNEY
OF THE EMBASSY

OF THE

DUTCH EAST-INDIA COMPANY
TO THE COURT OF THE EMPEROR OF CHINA,

IN THE YEARS 1794 AND 1795.

January 31, 1795.

THE Ambaffador and I fet off this morning at five o'clock in little carts, in order to repair to the Imperial refidence. It being too dark for the driver of mine to diftinguifh objects, he overturned me in a ditch, when we had been about half an hour on our way. Fortunately, as the ice was thick, I received no injury. I quitted the carriage, and got into the road. Another was provided for me, and my firft driver was difmiffed.

The Mandarins, our conductors, expreffed much fatisfaction at my not being hurt; for they are

are refponfible for any misfortunes we may experience, even fuch as affect our exiftence: for if any of us fhould accidentally lofe his life, he confequences of that event would be fuch as to endanger their own.

After being an hour on the road, we were conducted through a back gate within the walls. We were then fhewn into an apartment at no great diftance to the fouth, there to wait for break of day. That moment being come, we proceeded by a winding road, lined with large trees, towards a great open fpace in a wood, where a large tent of the Tartar kind, in the form of a dome, had been pitched for the Emperor. A fquare yellow tent was erected in the front of the other, while fix little bell-tents, which ftood on the two fides, were deftined for the Minifters and Grandees of the Court.

The Emperor's tent was exactly fimilar in the infide to the halls which I have feveral times had occafion to mention, and in the middle was an eftrade and a throne. I remarked that the inftruments and other appendages of the mufic had been conveyed hither from *Pe-king*.

His Majefty came a little after fun-rife in a palanquin

palanquin borne by four Mandarins of the gold button. He alighted under the yellow tent, and went on foot to his arm-chair. As foon as he was feated, all the guefts performed the falute of honour. The Envoys fat upon cufhions placed upon a carpet under the yellow tent in front of the Emperor's, with little breakfaft-tables before them as at the preceding *fêtes*.

After the Emperor's table was ferved, the fmall tables were likewife uncovered, each confifting of fifty difhes, as on the 20th of this month. I perceived all the guefts fall to with a great deal of eagernefs and appetite, while we contented ourfelves with a little fruit, and with viewing the reft of the company. His Majefty again fent us a difh from his, and fhortly after a difh of the milk of beans was prefented to each of the guefts.

The Emperor's breakfaft being over, we went with the three Corean Ambaffadors to repeat, as upon former occafions, the falute of honour before the throne, with our heads covered. His Majefty himfelf then prefented us with a glafs of Chinefe wine, with the tafte of which I was much pleafed. He afked the Ambaffador if he were not very cold, and enquired of me, whether in the whole courfe of my life I had ever been prefent at fuch ceremonies before.' As foon as the interpreter had conveyed to him our anfwers, we returned to our feats.

While all this was paffing, the orcheftra executed feveral pieces of mufic; feats of fleight and activity were performed; and at a little diftance a play was reprefented. Thefe various entertainments produced a confufion that foon fatigued the mind, and banifhed every idea of amufement.

The Emperor being gone, every one rofe and followed his example. We were then conducted towards a ferpentine canal, there to wait for the arrival of the two principal Minifters, who were not long before they made their appearance. We advanced a few fteps to meet them, and faluted them in the European manner.

The *Voo-tchong-tang* fpoke to us with the greateft air of kindnefs, and gave orders for our being conducted to the place whither he was going himfelf. He fet off upon a fled, and we followed him in another. After being drawn a confiderable diftance, we came to the front of a building which the Minifters entered. We alfo alighted and followed them, paffing through

feveral

several apartments which, according to the Chinese custom, constantly opened into each other. They were all decently furnished.

Upon coming to a little pool that was entirely thawed, the Ministers stopped to make us remark a number of gold fish of an extraordinary size; for the smallest was about fifteen inches long, and the rest a great deal larger. We were assured that these beautiful animals were exceedingly old.

Hence we were shewn into all the little apartments which constitute the Emperor's daily habitation. They are very numerous, of small dimensions, neatly furnished in the Chinese taste, and containing a few books and some very valuable curiosities. Three only of these apartments can boast of European time-pieces. Each room has a sofa for the Monarch, as also a couple of stools, but no such thing as a chair.

After having examined this edifice, the Prime Minister ordered the *Naa-fan-tayen* to carry us to see some other buildings. We then took leave of that worthy Minister, in order to follow our conductor.

After a quarter of an hour's walk along a high road, we came to a vaſt and magnificent palace, in the front of which is a very extenſive ſquare. On each ſide of this ſquare is a ſpacious paved court, correſponding with one of the wings of the building. Theſe wings ſeem intended as lodgings for the officers of the court, and the inferior Mandarins. Two pedeſtals of white marble ſtand in the middle of the court-yards, and ſupport two very large bronze lions, which may be conſidered as well executed by the artiſt, becauſe they accord with the idea that the Chineſe form of that animal, which is entirely unknown in their country.

The firſt hall in the front of the building is very large, and hung with a great many lanterns, in the Chineſe faſhion. In the middle of it, as in the other halls I have deſcribed, is an eſtrade, and an arm-chair, or Imperial throne. After having croſſed this hall, we found ourſelves in an inner paved court, of a ſquare form. The buildings on the north and weſt ſides of this court afford as rich and as beautiful a view as the eaſtern facade we firſt came to; while on the ſouth ſide there is nothing but a great gate leading into it, with offices for ſervants at each end.

Within

Within this gate, which corresponds with the north front, stands, as it were to mask it, a large rock of one entire piece upon a number of stones that serve it as a base. The carriage of this rock must have occasioned immense trouble and labour, as well as the operation of placing it upon its base; for its bulk and weight constitute a prodigious mass. Every side of it is honoured with inscriptions in the Emperor's own hand, and in that of several other persons of the highest rank who have imitated the example of the Monarch. In several parts of it are also dwarf trees and flowers.

Within this court, at the middle of the north front, stand two little stags, and two cranes, all of bronze, and of indifferent execution. The north side of the building contains an Imperial audience chamber with a throne in the centre, and lanterns in every part. Our conductor pointed out to us the coach of which Lord Macartney made a present to the Emperor last year, standing against the wall on the left side of the throne. It is exquisitely painted, perfectly well varnished, and the whole of the carriage is covered with gilding. The harness and the rest of the equipage are in the body of the coach, which is covered with a linen cloth. I perceived on the

opposite

oppofite fide of the hall a thing which made a remarkable contraſt with this fplendid vehicle, that is to fay a Chinefe waggon with four wheels of equal height, very clumfy, painted green all over, and in every refpect refembling the waggons ufed in Holland for the purpofe of carrying manure.

I confefs this fight fet my imagination to work. Was this waggon placed here with a view of oppofing the idea of its utility to that of the fuperfluity of a carriage fo fumptuous, at leaft according to the eſtimation of the Chinefe? I was thus giving way to my conjectures, when I was told that the waggon is the very fame that is made ufe of at the annual ceremony when the Emperor pays a folemn homage to agriculture in the Temple of the Earth. Behind this hall are feveral fmall apartments which the Emperor occupies when refident here.

After paffing through thofe apartments we came to the third range of buildings or weftern edifice which has only a fmall hall in the centre. The remainder is compofed of a great number of little confined and irregular rooms, opening into one another, and forming all together a fort of labyrinth.

When

When we had infpected the whole of them, the Mandarin ufhered us into the favourite cabinet of the Emperor, which bears the name of *Tien* (Heaven). It is indeed the moft agreeable place of thofe that have been fhewn us; as well on account of its fituation, as of the different views which it commands. Nothing can equal the profpect that the Emperor may enjoy when, fitting in his arm-chair, he turns his eyes towards a large window confifting of a fingle pane of glafs—a profpect of which the reader will himfelf be able to form an idea from the fequel of this defcription. This cabinet is in a part of the building fituated upon an extenfive lake which wafhes its walls.

This lake was the firft object that attracted our attention. In the midft of it is an ifland of confiderable magnitude, on which feveral buildings have been erected that are dependencies of this Imperial refidence, and overfhadowed by lofty trees. The ifland communicates with the adjacent continent by a noble bridge of feventeen arches, built of hewn ftone, and ftanding on the eaftern fide. This bridge was the next thing that our eyes refted upon.

Turning

Turning to the weftward, the fight is gratified by the view of a lake fmaller than the former, and only feparated from it by a wide road. In the midft of it is a kind of citadel of a circular form, with a handfome edifice in its centre. Thefe two lakes communicate by a channel cut through the road that divides them, while a ftone bridge of confiderable height, and of a fingle arch, fupplies the defect in the communication by land which that channel occafions.

Still further to the weftward, and at a great diftance, the eye is arrefted by two towers ftanding on the tops of lofty mountains.

To the north-weft ftands a magnificent range of edifices belonging to temples, conftructed at the foot, in the middle, and upon the fummit of a mountain entirely formed by art, with fragments of natural rocks, which, independently of the expence of the buildings, muft have coft immenfe fums, fince this kind of ftone is only to be found at a great diftance from the place. This work feems to reprefent the enterprize of the giants who attempted to fcale the Heavens: at leaft rocks heaped upon rocks recal that ancient fiction to the mind. The affemblage of the buildings and picturefque embellifhments of the

mountains

mountains afford a view of which the pen can give no adequate idea. It is not then without reaſon that this cabinet is the favourite apartment of the aged Monarch.

The inſide of it is furniſhed with a library, and ſhelves on which are collected all the moſt valuable and ſcarce Chineſe productions, conſiſting both of precious ſtones and antiques; and certainly they are highly deſerving of the attention with which we examined them.

After having paſſed a conſiderable time in this building with real pleaſure, we came to the ſouth front, where we found a ſled, which conveyed us towards the Temples that I have mentioned above.

They are five ſeparate pagodas; two are at the foot of the mountain; one fronting the north, the other the ſouth. Two others are ſituated near its middle and in the ſame poſition; and the fifth is upon its ſummit.

The lower temple fronting the ſouth contains an idol, which is the image of ſenſuality. It is very large, and entirely gilt. It repreſents a perſon of enormous corpulence, ſitting upon a cuſhion,

cushion, with an air expressive of satisfaction and gaiety. In this pagoda there are besides a great number of other idols, but of smaller dimensions and less importance.

In the south temple in the middle of the mountain, the principal idol is the figure of a woman, about sixty feet high, with six faces and a thousand arms, like that of the Temple of *Tay-say-tin* at *Pe-king*, of which I made mention the day before yesterday.

This temple forms, as it were, a nave and two aisles, by means of two rows of supports or pillars standing lengthwise. All along both the walls and the pillars are imitations of rocks, with cavities containing idols and saints by hundreds, and composing altogether a spectacle of a very singular and striking kind.

From this part of the mountain to which we had ascended by at least a hundred and twenty steps, we climbed towards its summit by means of a path winding between rocks, and of forty eight more steps, the shortest of which were a foot in height. Hence we discovered *Pe-king* in the south-east, and in the intermediate ground could distinguish several habitations or establish-
ments,

ments, which are fo many dependencies of *Yuen-ming-yuen.*

The fifth temple is upon the fummit of the mountain; its conftruction is in many refpects fimilar to that of a tower, and in it we found three images in a fitting pofture of enormous fize, and entirely gilt. Thefe are the principal idols of the temple. In one of the lower ftories, and oppofite thefe great images, are nine goddeffes alfo fitting and gilt, but much fmaller, while on each fide are nine bronze ftatues of faints, all of coloffal fize, and very well executed.

The walls behind the great idols are covered from one end to the other by large pannels, each of which contains feveral hundred figures of gods made of bronze, and placed in fmall niches. The outer walls of the temple are coated with varnifhed bricks, fuch as I have defcribed in fpeaking of the Temple of *Houing-ou-tzu* in the Imperial palace of *Pe king*, and having like thofe of that temple the figure of a *Jos* in *bas-relief* in the middle.

Having taken a fufficient view of this laft temple, we defcended the north fide of the mountain by fteps of rugged ftones, and came to the

temple

temple mid-way up the mountain, and fronting the north. Its principal idol is gilt all over, and reprefents a goddefs with a number of arms. The lower part of this temple, like the fecond which we vifited, is divided into three portions; and on the walls and pillars are an imitation of clouds, full of images of *Jos*, which produce upon the whole a pleafing effect.

From this temple we defcended to the lower one fronting the north, in which is a colloffal goddefs about ninety feet high, with four faces and forty-four arms. On each fide, but ftanding a little forwarder, are two other idols, at leaft forty-five feet high, and feeming to adore the goddefs. In this temple are alfo two fuperb quadrangular pyramids ftanding upon marble pedeftals, the fides of which are covered with *Jos* of bronze.

The inner wall is entirely coated with bricks, enriched with flowers in *bas-relief* of different colours, and all of them varnifhed. Againft the wall ftand columns, the fhafts of which rifing fix feet above the bafe are coated with bronze.

The five temples contain befides vafes for perfumes and other facred utenfils all of bronze,
and

and exquifitely wrought. There is not a fingle one among them that for beauty of fubject and delicacy of workmanfhip may not be juftly compared with thofe that are to be feen in the temples at *Pe-king.*

Each of thefe temples has alfo a fore-court and a portico, with fome marble decorations in the interior of the court.

Upon the top of the rocks piled upon one another in the ftupendous manner I have mentioned, are two fquare open pavilions of fymmetrical conftruction, as well as two little houfes in the fhape of towers, and feveral other fmall apartments. Their roofs are embellifhed with varnifhed tiles, green, blue, and yellow; fometimes difpofed in fquares or compartments in which thofe various tints are combined, or elfe being of one and the fame colour. Some of thefe little buildings are even coated on the outfide with fmooth fquare tiles fo varnifhed that when the fun ftrikes upon them they reflect all the fplendor of his beams.

But inftead of rafhly undertaking to exprefs and defcribe with my weak pen all that my eyes admired; inftead of endeavouring to communicate to my reader's mind, the many, the varied and

and the extraordinary fenfations produced incef-
fantly in mine by the fight of fo many things, in
which fingularity, magnificence, boldnefs of de-
fign, and fkill of execution were combined, it
will be more fimple and more natural to confefs
my incapability. The pencil of a great mafter
is wanting to create in fome fort anew fo many
accumulated wonders, and even then I will
venture to fay, without feeking to fave my own
credit, that the copy will never be equal to the
original.

With what pleafure would I have facrificed
a fum of money to obtain a plan, and a dozen of
the moft interefting views of this magnificent
fummer palace. For to try to give by defcription
an idea of Chinefe architecture, particularly that
of the Imperial refidence, would be a fruitlefs endeavour, and almoft a lofs of time, the mode of
conftruction in that country not having the
fmalleft analogy with European architecture.
I am indeed fo much convinced that every defcription of that kind, unaffifted by drawings,
would not be underftood, that I fhall abandon the
attempt.

On quitting the pagodas we were led along a
very pleafant winding road, neatly paved with
little

little pebbles, overshadowed by trees, passing sometimes over hills, and sometimes through vallies; such a road in short, as in summer, when every thing is green, must make a most delightful promenade.

After a few minutes walk we came to a groupe of small buildings inclosed within the walls of an Imperial palace which overlooks them, being as much superior to them in height as it exceeds them in size. They form a kind of village, in the midst of which runs a stream of very limpid water, skirted with small rocks on each side, and at this moment free from ice. These buildings are not inhabited at present, but during summer, when his Majesty makes *Yuen-ming-yuen* his residence, they serve as shops for tradesmen of all sorts, who come there to sell their goods, and compose something not unlike one of our fairs. It is possible that this place may then be very lively and amusing, and that the water that runs through it may at once furnish the means of cleanliness, and serve to keep it cool.

Thence we were conducted towards another assemblage of buildings, where the *Voo-tchong-tang* waited for us in one of the halls. We advanced towards him, and paid him our compliments

ments, accompanied by a genuflexion. For this Prime Minifter, this firft agent of the Empire, is called, as I have before obferved, THE SECOND EMPEROR; and in fome refpects the Chinefe pay almoft as much honour to him as to the Emperor himfelf: nobody dares fpeak to him without bending the knee. He received us with an affability which had all the characteriftics of fincerity, and afked us our opinion of what we had feen. Our interpreter conveyed to him the expreffion of our pleafure, our fatisfaction, and our well-grounded aftonifhment, and above all, our praife of his Majefty's little cabinet. The Prime Minifter then told us that the Emperor, being exceedingly pleafed with the perfons felected for the Dutch Embaffy, had wifhed to give us a proof of his favour and affection, by granting more to us than to any other foreigner, fince the foot of an alien had never before trod in the private apartments of his Majefty, nor had any European eye ever perceived what we had been permitted to examine; that very few even of the natives of the country were fortunate enough to approach thofe places; and that we might thence judge how far the Monarch had carried his preference and predilection. We endeavoured on our part to fhew our high fenfe of the honour
done

done us, and the greatnefs of our refpectful gratitude.

To give us a mark of ftill farther favour, the Prime Minifter made us a prefent in the name of the Emperor. That for the Ambaffador confifted of four rolls of filk, feveral embroidered purfes to hold tobacco, a fmall bottle for fnuff, and two porringers of porcelain. Mine was the fame, except that I had only two rolls of filk. We returned our thanks by performing the falute of honour.

The Prime Minifter then made us fit down oppofite him upon cufhions laid on the ground, and paftry and fweetmeats were handed to us. Upon tafting fome of them we found them as good as we could have defired in Europe. We were afterwards prefented with a difh of tea.

His Excellency and I then rofe, and approaching the Minifter, the Ambaffador again offered him in the name of our Prince, and of the Dutch Eaft-India Company, the prefents that were intended for him, entreating him to accept them, according to the example of the Prime Minifters, at the time of the other Dutch Embaffies. He anfwered in a very kind manner; but perfifted in his

his refusal by saying that it would ill become him to take gifts presented by those who had already suffered so much fatigue in so long a journey; and added, that he begged us to excuse his not accepting our offers, and to spare him any new solicitations on the subject.

His Excellency on this abstained from any farther mention of presents; but he requested another favour, that of returning to *Canton* by water. The *Voo-tchong-tang* very graciously promised us his intercession with the Emperor. We then returned to our places, and again took some refreshments in consequence of the pressing entreaties of the Prime Minister.

He sent us his watch, desiring us to let him know what we thought of it. As it was made by Arnold, we had it in our power to praise it without flattery. The *Voo-tchong-tang* then desired to see ours; and afterwards spoke of the high price of some watches in the possession of our mechanist, which he said he should be glad to buy at an easier rate, observing at the same time that his only cost him three hundred and seventy-five livres. It would have been easy for us to give him a very intelligible explanation of this low price; but the fear of the consequences that might

might have attended it in refpect to the tranfactions of the Mandarins and merchants of Canton, and particularly the rifk that might be run by the former, prevented me from going into particulars; and we contented ourfelves with expreffing our furprize at fuch a watch being procured for fo fmall a fum.

When the converfation had lafted a few minutes longer the Prime Minifter rofe; we did the fame; and then after taking a friendly leave he left us. The paftry and fweetmeats that remained on our tables were put into our handkerchiefs and delivered to our fervants.

On going hence we paffed along a winding and ftony road, by the fide of which runs murmuring along a ftream of the moft pellucid water. After a few turns we came to a building near a back gate, where our carts were waiting for us.

There we left the *Naa-fan-tayen*, after having thanked him for accompanying us with fo much complaifance; then, feating ourfelves in our fplendid cars, we drove to our lodgings. As our return took place during the day, we remarked that we were paffing along a large place compofed of feveral ftreets entirely lined with handsome shops, which, added to the crouds passing to and fro, furnished a presumption of considerable commerce.

It was a quarter past eleven when we got back to our hotel, exceedingly well pleased with the agreeable and unexpected excursion we had been making for the last two hours and a quarter. I only regretted that the rest of the party had not partaken of our pleasure.

I endeavoured even to discover the reason of their exclusion, and was told that apprehensions were entertained lest M. Agie, our French interpreter, who understands the Mandarin language too well, at least for the interest of our Mandarins, should be dangerous if, in conversing with him, too nice enquiries should be made concerning many things relative to Canton. This is the reason of their taking so much care to let nobody but the Ambassador and myself appear at court. Perhaps there would have been no objection to including in the number of the favourites of the day the three Dutch gentlemen in the suite of the Embassy, if it would not have been too clearly marking the exclusion of the others, and a breach of all decorum. It was, therefore, deemed most prudent to admit nobody but his Excellency and me me into thefe extraordinary parties, which were a diftinguifhed mark of his Majefty's favour. I am, however, promifed, that all our gentlemen fhall be prefent at an entertainment and fireworks that are to take place on a very early day.

From the tenor of the *Voo-tchong-tang's* difcourfe this morning, I fee plainly that the court is not acquainted with the underhand dealings of the Mandarins at Canton; and I doubt not but the merchants who manage the affairs of the *Cohang* are concerned in thofe intrigues. It is certain that even in London Arnold never fold a watch for three hundred and feventy-five livres, and that no Chinefe merchant could be able to procure one at Canton for lefs than fix or eight times that fum. But to pay their court to the Mandarins, and particularly to the *Hou-pou*, who is a kind of god in their eyes, and who is charged by the Grandees of the Empire to procure them European merchandize, they part with commodities at a price inferior to their value, and give receipts which are fent to *Pe-king* with the articles purchafed. Hence it refults that the Emperor and the great perfonages about court are perfectly ignorant of the real price of things executed by the celebrated artifts of Europe. If, indeed, it were otherwife, would the Prime Minifter

Minifter have told us with fo much candour what he had paid for his watch and other trinkets which he fhewed us with that fimplicity which characterizes truth.

I muft obferve that the Minifters of State never accept a prefent from any one whatever, without the exprefs permiffion of the Emperor. It is confequently proper that they fhould have receipts for every thing they procure.

But it is well known that the *Cohang* has a particular fund at Canton, arifing from the duties paid on all goods imported or exported by Europeans, except woollen cloth and other manufactured articles. Thefe duties were eftablifhed in 1779 by the *Tfong-tou*, for the following reafon:

An Englifh fhip of war, called the Seahorfe, commanded by Captain Panton, being come to Canton to enforce the definitive recovery of what was due to Britifh merchants from three or four great Chinefe houfes which had failed; a recovery which the Englifh fupercargoes were never able to effect by their own applications, it was thought proper to lay on a tax for ten years in order to extinguifh the debt. But the impoft has

has furvived the motive of its creation, the duties ftill continuing to be received.

It is from thefe receipts that the merchants, without any lofs to themfelves, affect to be generous, and give the Mandarins the moft valuable things for a trifle, being fure to find in the fund a ready indemnity.

It is, then, eafy to conceive that the great prefents made by the merchants to the Mandarins, coft them abfolutely nothing; but that they are made at the expence of the Europeans, whofe merchandize ftill continues to be oppreffed by a tax which ought no longer to exift. It is furprifing that a general demand for its fuppreffion has not been made; for although this impoft appears indirect, its effect is not lefs real than that of an impoft upon bread, which falls upon the poor although they buy it of the baker, who fays not a word to them of the tax.

I think, however, that every reprefentation would be ufelefs unlefs it were fupported like the demand of the Englifh; for both Mandarins and merchants find in this abufe the means of fatisfying their thirft after gain. It would, indeed, be impoffible for the latter to comply with
the

the interested views of the former if such a source were dried up. A system of corruption so well contrived must necessarily continue to exist, and to acquire new strength every day, till it reaches those limits when the abuse, become monstrous and pernicious in the extreme, both to commerce and traders, shall call for reform in a manner too imperative to be despised.

February 1. This day has been a day of repose, and, for the first time for a great while past, we have enjoyed the blessing of an uninterrupted night's rest.

The Mandarin, our conductor, came about noon to give us notice to hold ourselves in readiness to go to-morrow at twelve o'clock to court, where we shall probably stay till the evening is far advanced. He advised us to dine before our departure, that we might afterwards be the more masters of our time.

Every day our conductors become more and more polite, and redouble their attention, because they perceive with what distinction their monarch treats us, and with what kindness he wishes to procure us frequent enjoyments. Convinced that they are so many marks of high favour,

favour, they take from them, as it were, the meafure of what is due to our character, it being notorious to every one that his Majefty is exceedingly well fatisfied with the Embaffy, and with the conduct of thofe belonging to it. I can atteft that he never paffed in his palanquin by any place where we were, without turning his eyes towards us with a look expreffive of kindnefs, which is one of the moft marked attentions that the manners of China would permit him to fhew us.

2d. Although our conductors had urged our dining at an early hour, we did not leave our lodgings till paft three o'clock. After having been driven three quarters of an hour in a carriage, we were conducted through a great gate into a wood, in which were pitched feveral round tents of the Tartarian kind. We were placed in one of them to wait for the Emperor's arrival, who came a little before five o'clock, and feated himfelf in a kind of niche in the centre of the building.

That building confifts of two ftories, the upper one of which is occupied by the females of the Emperor's family. But in point of conftruction it is the leaft remarkable of any we have yet
feen,

seen, nothing about it befpeaking an Imperial refidence. There were openings of a fingle pane of glafs in the windows for the ladies to peep through in order to fee into the fquare, in the midft of which the building ftands. This fquare, called *San-cou-chui-tchung*, is the fame in which the Emperor's tent was erected the day before yefterday.

A little before his Majefty's arrival we were defired to fit down upon cufhions, laid flat on carpets covering the ground, in order to fee the fireworks. Some wreftlers, tumblers, muficians, and a miferable rope-dancer amufed the old Monarch with their tirefome performances, which were of fo wretched a kind, that in Europe they would hardly have attracted any fpectators whatever.

At half paft five preparations began to be made for the exhibition of the fireworks. The whole was brought in two great and two fmall covered waggons, the former containing three great pieces each; the latter a fingle piece, confifting of a great number of lanterns. There were, befides, a great many wheels, ferpents, and other fireworks, but no rockets. The pieces brought in the great covered waggons were very pretty,

pretty, and were alone deferving of attention, the reft not being comparable to European productions of the fame kind. It is, befides, matter of regret that fireworks fhould be exhibited in the day-time, the light deftroying their moft brilliant effects; but the old Monarch is fo much afraid of fire, that he will never permit any to be difplayed during the night. Even at thefe two little European fire-engines were ready, as well as a great number of tubs full of water, and pails, to extinguifh the burning paper of the crackers, as foon as their explofion fhould be at end.

A little after fix o'clock the whole was over, and we returned to our hotel, whither a meffenger came to give notice to his Excellency and me to prepare again to go at an early hour tomorrow to court, where we were expected to breakfaft.

3d. We were on our way to court at four o'clock in the morning. While waiting for daylight to appear we firft ftopped in a little apartment, and afterwards walked towards a magnificent edifice, which we had not yet feen, and in front of which is a large open fquare. It has a great refemblance to the fecond building that we vifited on the 31ft of January. It has alfo a court-yard, court-yard, in which ſtand two lions of bronze upon pedeſtals of marble, but they are ſmaller than thoſe of the other edifice.

From this open ſpace or eſplanade we were conducted through a very large gate with three paſſages, into a court in the front of it entirely paved with ſmooth ſtones. The gate itſelf is an edifice two ſtories high; is of the ſame conſtruction and magnitude; and is laid out in the ſame manner as that of the palace of *Pe-king*, of which I made mention on the 20th of January, except that here the hall called *Tjing-tay-quong-ming* is paved with white marble, as well as the front gallery, at the two ends of which are alſo placed all manner of muſical inſtruments. The hall is hung round with Chineſe lanterns of various ſhapes.

At ſun-riſe the *Voo-tchong-tang* entered, and came immediately towards us to inform the Ambaſſador that his Majeſty had given orders that on our return we ſhould travel for the firſt eighteen days over land, and afterwards entirely by water; but that during the whole journey we ſhould be conducted in any way we might prefer, and be provided with all poſſible accommodations. We thanked him for this arrangement,

againſt

againſt which we had not the ſmalleſt objection to make.

He afterwards went to the inner part of the hall, where the Emperor, who ſoon after made his appearance, ſeated himſelf in his arm-chair. The ceremonial, entertainments, muſic, little tables of fifty diſhes, every thing in ſhort was the ſame as the day before yeſterday. We had, however, to-day a ſerious dance, which had not taken place at the former feſtivals. It was executed by a ſet of Mandarins, who firſt advanced two by two, and afterwards made ſome meaſured movements with their arms and feet, keeping time with the muſic, but without ſhifting their ground, and only turning round upon that which they occupied. Each pair of dancers exerciſed themſelves in this way for about three minutes, after which they performed the ſalute of honour and retired.

Theſe Mandarins were all dreſſed in the ſame manner. The buttons on their caps were oval, hexagonal, and of different colours, blue, white, and coraline. The caps had a thick covering of very fine raw ſilk; and from the hind part a kind of flap or hood fell back upon their ſhoulders. Round their necks they wore ſeveral rows

of

of large beads, hanging down to the breaft. I afked of what rank they were, and here follows what I was able to collect:

They are called *Chiouais*, and are a body folely compofed of the fons of the principal Mandarins of the Empire, fuch as the *Tfong-tous*, the *Tay-toys*, the *Fou-yuens*, and others of the firft rank. They are taught the military art, and ought to underftand the ufe of the bow and arrow to perfection. The firft clafs is the *Yuchin-Chiouais*, who guard the doors of the exterior of the palace, and always remain near the Emperor's perfon: their button is of red coral. The fecond clafs confifts of the *Tinchin-Chiouais* to whofe care the external gates of the palace are entrufted: their button is dark blue. Laft comes the third clafs, or common *Chiouais*, who are armed with bows and arrows, and accompany the Emperor's palanquin, either on foot or horfeback, whenever he makes a long excurfion. Their button is of a dull and milky white.

The object of their dance is an homage which they pay once a year to the Emperor in this place; fhewing, by the movements of their arms, that they are always ready to defend his power and protect his perfon.

There

There seems to be a great conformity between this body of Mandarins and the perfons who in the courts of Europe are ftyled chamberlains, gentlemen in waiting, and body-guards; comparing to each rank one of the claffes of *Chiouais*. The two firft of thefe have their pofts of honour like the chamberlains and gentlemen in waiting, while the third ferve in the fame capacity as body guards. It was the latter who efcorted the Emperor on horfeback with their bows and arrows when he was going to the Temple of Heaven on the 27th of January, and when he returned on the following day.

I am now, then, enabled to fay, that his Imperial Majefty has a body of life guards, which I did not before imagine, never having feen in attendance upon him any perfons armed even with fabres. Every body goes to court without arms. We never even appeared there with our fwords, leaving them at our hotel in conformity with the wifh expreffed by the Mandarins in confequence of the Emperor's orders.

Once only I faw the *Chiouais* appear in a body before the Emperor with their fwords by their fide. This was on the 20th of January, and their drefs was then entirely different, being clofe

clofe and richly embroidered wtth dragons of gold, which gave them a very magnificent appearance.

To-day the two principal Minifters had their fabres by their fides for a few minutes at the time of the Emperor's arrival ; but in general no military Mandarin wears his fword as a mark of his office, unlefs when in the field, whereas in Europe an officer is always obliged to appear with arms.

At court the Mandarins wear no diftinctive mark except that which is embroidered alike upon the breaft and back of their robes. It confifts of lions and dragons for the military Mandarins, and of cranes, ftags, and herons for Mandarins of letters. Hence the department to which they belong is known. It is from the body of the *Chiouais,* that the greater number of Mandarins are taken for the provinces, where they are appointed to military employs, and in general they rife to the higheft dignities of their profeflion.

We were to-day taken once more to the foot of the throne, where we received a glafs of wine from the Monarch's own hand, after which we returned

returned to our places. Soon after the Emperor arofe, which terminated every thing, and we returned to our lodgings. We got there at a quarter paft nine.

The reafon which prevents our returning entirely by water is the idea that there will not be a thaw, in lefs than fix weeks, fufficient to render the rivers navigable; and that our ftay, if prolonged to the end of that time, would be too long in itfelf, and tirefome to us, who are kept in a fort of confinement. We fhall then take in part a different route from that which brought us to *Pe-king*, and fhall pafs through the province of *Shan-tong*, which, independent of variety, will procure us a fight of regions whither as yet no foreigner has penetrated. We fhall take every day as the meafure of our journey's duration, that of the fun above the horizon, and at *Vou-ca-fou*, which is two day's journey within the province of *Kiang-nam*, we fhall embark. Such is the outline of the report made to us this day by one of our Canton Mandarins.

We are eafily reconciled to the idea of thefe new fatigues, and prefer a fpeedy end to our captivity to all the attentions which are lavifhed upon us here. O delightful liberty! we do not begin to

be

be fenfible of thy value till threatened with the lofs of thine ineftimable enjoyments.

I this day received a letter from my friend Grammont, to whom I returned an anfwer immediately. He is ftill in hopes of feeing us fhortly.

This afternoon, at three o'clock, our whole party went again to court to fee an exhibition of fireworks; but as the wind was high, a meffenger was fent to us, after half an hour had elapfed, to fay that his Majefty had fufpended the feftival for that evening. We fet off directly for our lodgings.

Having obtained at Canton from the merchant Paonkequa twenty drawings, confifting of views of *Yuen-ming-yuen,* in order to copy them, I was naturally furprized, after finding among them reprefentations of edifices built and laid out in the European manner, to find none of the fame kind at *Yuen-ming-yuen* itfelf. I therefore afked our conductors if fuch buildings did really exift? They told me in anfwer that they did; that they were ten *li* diftance from *Hoi-tim,* the place where we now are; and that they are occupied by part of the Emperor's wives. Upon my enquiring

whether

whether we could not go to fee them, I was told that I muft beg the *Naa-fan-tayen* to afk permiffion of the *Voo-tchong-tang*. I mean to take the firft favourable opportunity to obtain that pleafure, if poffible.

We had alfo an idea of paying a vifit to the great walls or rampart of China; but hearing that they are two hundred *li* off, we fhall not make the requeft, becaufe it is probable that the trouble fo long a journey would occafion might make our obtaining permiffion a matter of doubt.

4th. This is a day of reft, as to us, on account of an eclipfe of the moon, which obliges the Emperor and all the grandees of the Empire to retire into their inner apartments, and put on mourning. His Majefty on fuch occafions is entirely taken up with the performance of fome pious rites in favour of the Sun or Moon, in order to refcue them from the dreadful fate with which they are threatened by the great dragon, who obfcures the fplendor of one or other of thofe planets, by holding them in his mouth with the intention of fwallowing them. The Chinefe perfift in this miferable fuperftition, to which they have been addicted from time immemorial, although the moft plain demonftrations of a pla-
netarium

netarium fhow them that the event is natural, and the eclipfes of the moon are caufed by the interpofition of the earth between the fun and moon while the latter is at the full; in like manner as the eclipfes of the fun are produced at the time of the new moon, by its interpofition between the fun and the earth. But the attachment of this nation for the ideas of its anceftors, and its veneration for the commandments it has received from them, are fo ftrong, that a fon never dares to appear more learned than his father. It is from this rule of its ancient philofophers, which fhould rather be taken in a figurative than a literal fenfe, that refults its little progrefs in all the fciences, and its blind attachment to old cuftoms.

It is evident that the fcientific knowledge poffeffed by the Chinefe is of very ancient date, and that they obtained it long before the fciences were known in Europe. But every thing has remained in its primitive ftate, without their ever feeking, like the Europeans, to make farther progrefs, or to bring their difcoveries to perfection. We have confequently far furpaffed them. Nor can a doubt be entertained of their perceiving it; but they are utterly regardlefs of this fuperiority. Fully fatisfied with their fum of intelligence; perfuaded that it fuffices for all the wants of their exiftence; and confidering our advance towards perfection as ufelefs, and abfolutely fuperfluous, they are refolved to make no attempts to follow us. Befides, in doing fo, they would be obliged to violate the precept I have already mentioned.

I muft once more obferve, that there is no nation fo fervilely attached to the ufages and maxims of its anceftors as the Chinefe. And we fhall ceafe to be aftonifhed at it, when we know that filial refpect is without bounds among them; that this tie of nature ftands in the ftead of legifla- tion, the place of which it entirely fupplies; and that their great philofopher *Kong-fou-tfé*, by deduc- ing all his principles of family relations from thofe between father and fon, found means to acquire an authority, which ferved in its turn to ftrengthen that firft natural fentiment, that primary founda- tion of every focial fyftem. And does it not feem as if the divine blefling promifed by the commandment that requires the children of Ifrael to honour their parents, were become the portion of the Chinefe! It is alfo in the execu- tion of this facred law, that, according to my weak judgment, we ought to feek the caufe of the long duration of this nation, the only one, excepting the

Japanefe

Japanese (subject also to the strict observance of the same precept), which has preserved itself the same from a period which is lost in the most remote antiquity.

In the rest of the universe, Empires have disappeared after having been overthrown and destroyed, and the greater part of them have only left an empty name, and the sterile renown of a splendour which is no more. In China, on the contrary, even the change of dynasty, by transferring the power to a Tartarian prince, did not change the nation. The conqueror, guided by a wise principle, instead of introducing the laws of his country, adopted those of the conquered, and thus becoming a Chinese himself, the Chinese nation was preserved entire by keeping its name, its language, and its manners. The Tartars, on their side, have remained a separate people, a kind of distinct empire, and enjoy to this day their own language and their own laws.

We may suppose, with great reason, we may even go so far as to consider it as almost certain, that the Chinese will remain a flourishing people to the utmost limits of time that thought can reach; because nature herself must henceforth protect their country against all enterprizes and

all

all invasions, so that it is impossible to attack them with any hope of subjecting them to a foreign power, or of ruining their country.

To the north, inhospitable deserts of considerable extent refuse a passage to a numerous army and the immense train that follows it, because it affords them no means of subsistence. To the southward and eastward rivers of small depth of water deny access to a fleet, while narrow highways prevent the regular march of an army, however small, that may have landed upon the coast. It would not indeed find any thing like a road to penetrate into the interior of the country, but paths only fit for a single man on foot or horseback, and frequently interrupted by ditches, ravines, and rivers, which are so many means of protection. To the west the defence of China consists in inaccessible mountains and impenetrable woods.

Thus guarded on every side, the Chinese have no reason to fear the destructive consequences which have resulted from war to so many other nations. The only means then of disturbing them would be the keeping up of a secret understanding with a part of the nation; but the difficulty of their language is a still more unsurmountable obstacle

obstacle than all those which I have enumerated above. That language is an eternal barrier placed between them and the rest of mankind; and time, while adding century to century, cannot weaken it, unless by overturning the whole surface of the globe.

I do not mean that from these truths it should be inferred that the Chinese may make a jest with impunity of any attempt by the Europeans to compel them to make such reforms as are necessary to put a stop to the scandalous exactions and barefaced frauds of the Mandarins of Canton, which are so burdensome to the commerce of Europe; so far from it, I am of opinion that such a measure would be attended with but little trouble and expence, even if undertaken by a single nation. But I think it prudent not to explain myself more fully upon the subject, and to pass over in silence both the project and the plan.

5th. In the morning a great Mandarin came on the part of the Emperor with presents intended for our Prince the Stadtholder, the Ambassador, and me. We performed the salute of honour, to express our gratitude.

Our

Our firſt conductor from Canton alſo came to inform me that he had received orders from his Imperial Majeſty to take us back to that city, and that the Emperor had himſelf fixed our departure for the twenty-ſixth day of the moon (the fifteenth of the preſent month). Agreeably with his requeſt, I intimated this determination to the Ambaſſador.

As I am deſirous of ſeeing before our departure the edifices at *Yuen-ming-yuen* that are conſtructed in the European manner, I begged the Mandarin, our conductor, to ſolicit this favour in my name of the Prime Miniſter. He obſerved to me that theſe edifices, being occupied by the Emperor's wives, it was impoſſible for them to be ſhewn to us. I replied that our curioſity would be ſatisfied by only ſeeing the outſide, were it even at ſome diſtance, as we only wiſhed to have the ſatisfaction of ſaying that we had perceived them. He then promiſed me to uſe his intereſt with the *Voo-tchong-tang*.

Our court conductor made his appearance afterwards, to give us notice that our whole party was expected this afternoon at the palace to be ſpectators of the fireworks.

We

We set off in consequence for the same place as the last time, and again waited under a tent in the wood for half an'hour. Thence we were desired to go to the esplanade in front of the building, where we sat down. On the Emperor's arrrival, his Excellency and I were removed from the place where we were into the paved court, in which we were alone, while the Ambassador's suite remained on the esplanade without. The upper story of the building was again full of ladies.

After his Majesty had been seated a few moments, a cup of milk of beans was brought to him, and the same was afterwards presented to all the guests. The wrestlers, the musicians, and the tumblers, continued their exercises till sun-set, when the fireworks began, which differed little from those we had seen before, except that at the end there was a kind of sham fight performed at a small distance under the trees. Fireworks were directed by each party against the other, and made a report which imitated that of muskets, and even that of heavy artillery, in an astonishing manner. This part of the entertainment was in fact the most amusing, because it fully equalled the expectations of the spectators, and gave reason to regret that the effect was not

aided

aided by the darknefs of night. The whole was over before fix o'clock, and in half an hour after we had reached our home.

The Mandarin, who has the direction of our lodgings, told us that we were to fet off tomorrow morning for *Pe-king*; but that his Excellency and I were to return in two days to pay our refpects to the Emperor.

As there feems to be no inclination to fhew us any thing more of this Imperial refidence, we were very glad to return to *Pe-king*, becaufe our baggage was there, and our lodgings are more comfortable.

6th. At half paft fix we quitted *Hoi-tim*, and reached our hotel at half paft twelve. Having returned by the fame road we went, we had no opportunity of obferving any thing new, except that when we had gone about half way we paffed near a magnificent pagoda, by the fide of which is a convent and many circumjacent buildings, which have all the outward appearance of Imperial edifices. I was told that the great bell fo famous throughout China is kept in this place, which is called *Tay-chong-miao*.

Being

Being come to the city of *Pe-king* itself, we entered a street that we had not yet seen, at a part where another more considerable street intercepts it at right angles. A square has been formed out of this cross-way, by the erection of four triumphal arches, having three passages each, and adorned with a profusion of painting, gilding, and sculpture. These four triumphal arches, which correspond with the middle of the streets, stand opposite each other, and in a straight line with the houses of the two cross streets. The four buildings forming the angles of the square are of uniform construction, and two stories high; their fronts being also ornamented with painting and gilding. All these decorations give the place a very handsome appearance. As to the rest, there are here as well as in the other streets of *Pe-king* a great crowd, and little tents filled with every kind of merchandize.

After dinner, our court conductor came to tell me that his Excellency and I were to return the day after to-morrow to *Yuen-ming-yuen*, to wait upon the Emperor in the afternoon, and to return in the evening to *Pe-king*. I communicated this to the Ambassador.

Shortly

Shortly after we had a vifit from the *Naa-fan-tayen*. I begged him, fince our departure was fo near, to endeavour to obtain leave for us to have the Miffionaries at our hotel for the laft three days, particularly Meffrs. Grammont and Roux, the former of thofe two gentlemen being my intimate friend. He again promifed to do every thing in his power.

I alfo afked to fee the celebrated Chinefe bell, and he undertook to folicit the Prime Minifter's permiffion.

He then fhewed me a common fquare bottle which he had brought with him, and in which was a little wooden mill, turned by fine fand falling through a kind of funnel at the top of the bottle upon the ladle boards of the wheel. In fhort, it was one of thofe play-things which are to be found in a thoufand different fhapes, and to be purchafed for a trifle in a European fair. He afked me if I was acquainted with this piece of mechanifm? I told him that I had feen a great number, and of a much handfomer external form. He then afked me why we had brought nothing with us of the fame kind? I obferved in anfwer, that as in our country they only ferve for the amufement of children, we had

not

not fuppofed that they would give the leaft pleafure, or excite the fmalleft attention. He affured us of the contrary, and fpoke in the language of a man who thinks himfelf the poffeffor of a wonder. This opinion was even ftrengthened when I fet the mill a-going, by putting new fand in the fire, and by fhewing him that after all ran out how it might be brought to the top again by turning up the bottle. It is not at all improbable that thefe trifles would find a good market here, and that they would perhaps amufe the Emperor himfelf as much as the pieces of mechanifm that we brought with us to *Pe-king*.

Before he left me the *Naa-fan-tayen* affured me that he intended to write concerning me to the *Tfong-tou* and the *Hou-pou* of Canton, for which I expreffed myfelf highly grateful. He is even in hopes, as he told me, of being *Hou-pou* at Canton himfelf the enfuing year, and I affured him that I fincerely wifhed him to fill that employ.

After more than an hour's converfation, he took leave in the moft friendly manner, and I attended him as far as the inner door. This evening he fent a prefent of fruit and fweatmeats to the Ambaffador and me.

7th. Nothing

7th. Nothing remarkable : we only began to make our arrangements with our travelling conductors as to our departure and mode of conveyance. It was at laſt reſolved that his Excellency and I ſhould perform that part of our journey that lay over land in palanquins ; the five gentlemen of our party, the mechaniſt, and *maitre d'hotel*, on horſeback, and the reſt of the ſuite in carts, with all the baggage, for the carriage of which no *Coulis* were to be got here.

As far as I have been able to obſerve, there are only three ways of tranſporting goods ; namely, by carts, by barrows, and on dromedaries.

Dromedaries are here very numerous; but it did not appear to me that they carried ſo heavy burthens on their backs as the camels of Arabia and the weſtern parts of India. I have alſo obſerved that their pace is very ſlow, ſo that their conductor can follow them with eaſe : we out-travelled them in our palanquins. It ſeems that this is the pace in which they go upon a journey. In walking their great arched neck is always pendant, conſequently their head does not lean upon their humps ; and while upon the road they are conſtantly chewing the cud. At the lower part of their necks they have

have some long hair, as fine as silk ; and in some this hair is very bushy. It is precisely the same as that which is so much valued in Europe in the manufactories of camlet, and which we export from Turkey. All the rest of the hair of the dromedary or camel is too short for working or spinning.

One thing which struck me was, that the sole of the dromedary's foot is tender all over, and to such a degree, that when it is stretched out the inside resembles a kind of elastic cushion. Rugged or stony roads must then be extremely troublesome to these animals, since such roads seem to require a very hard substance. The manner in which the dromedary lies down is also somewhat singular, inasmuch as he supports himself on his fore knees, and does not suffer the lower part of his body to touch the ground. He has then his neck stretched out, and his head erect. I had no opportunity of making farther observations on this animal.

Our Chinese servants this day obtained permission to go into the city to buy whatever might be needful. They returned this evening, very sorry that this indulgence had been granted. Having been discovered to be strangers at *Peking*, the centinels in the streets put them into a guard

guard-houfe. They did not fail to declare that they were part of the retinue of the Dutch Embaffy, and that they were natives of Canton, begging at the fame time that the *Lingua* might be fent for, to bear witnefs to the truth of what they advanced; but as the difcovery of the truth did not enter into the calculation of thefe military knaves, they began to ftrip them, and accufed them of felling opium. Unfortunately each of the fervants had a few dollars prepared for his purchafes; and that was exactly what thefe faithful guards were in fearch of. Chains were already prepared to conduct them to prifon, which terrified them to fuch a degree, that although innocent they made a tender of money, in order to efcape from the plunderers, who at laft fold them their liberty for a dozen *piaftres*. I intended to communicate thefe facts to the Mandarin, but my fervant begged me not to do fo, as their liberty had been obtained by means of a compofition, which if known might give them, as well as others, a great deal of trouble. I therefore refolved to fay nothing upon the fubject; but here we fee that even a Chinefe is not in perfect fafety in his own country, and to what a degree a private foldier may moleft a man who does not belong to the place. What then fhould not we Europeans have had to dread, if leave had

had been given us to walk about. At any rate we could not have moved a ſtep in the ſtreets without being eſcorted by a guard of ſoldiers, on account of the curioſity of the multitude crowding round us on all ſides, as we experienced every day, even in the interior of the Imperial palaces. We have therefore reaſon to believe that it is from prudential motives that we are ſo cloſely guarded, in order to preſerve us from a thouſand affronts which might have been offered us by the dregs of the people. In what country indeed is it poſſible to controul the mob? Beſides, as the Mandarins are reſponſible for our lives and for our ſatisfaction, it is ſtill more eaſy to believe that ſo many precautions are dictated to them by their own intereſt.

8th. This morning at eleven o'clock the Ambaſſador and I fet off for the country houſe of *Yuen-ming-yuen*. In paſſing through the city we met with a very remarkable funeral. It was that of a Mandarin of the firſt rank. The body was conducted out of *Pe-king* with a conſiderable proceſſion and a great deal of pomp.

On arrival at one o'clock at *Yuen-ming-yuen*, we were conducted to an apartment where we had already been, and where we ſtaid at leaſt

two

two hours. In the mean time fome fragments were brought from the Emperor's table on difhes of maffy gold, which indicates that he is ferved in that metal. From this apartment we were taken to a tent, and an hour afterwards to the great Efplanade, in which the fireworks were ufually difplayed.

At four o'clock the Emperor came out of the building and feated himfelf in his arm chair in the niche. I had then an opportunity of feeing him walk fome diftance, and I was very much furprifed to find that he was exceedingly upright, and ftood in no need of fupport. When ftanding he appears younger and ftronger than when in a fitting pofture. His ftature exceeds the common height.

His Majefty being feated, all the Envoys were prefented to him, thofe of each nation going together: we were the third. After we had performed the falute of honour with our hats off, the Emperor, through the medium of the Prime Minifter, defired the Ambaffador to tell our Prince how we had found him on our arrival, the ftate in which we had left him, the manner in which we had been received and treated, and what we had feen in his palaces. His Excellency returned

returned thanks to the Emperor for all the favours conferred upon us, and expreſſed his wiſh that his reign, protracted to a diſtant period, might be attended by that happineſs which good princes deſerve. We then repeated the ſalute of honour, and returned to our ſeats.

The different Envoys having thus had a general audience of leave, a cup of bean milk was firſt preſented to the Emperor, and afterwards handed round to all the gueſts.

A little table was afterwards prepared for us of paſtry and ſweetmeats, which rendered a diſh of mutton ſerved up at the ſame time a ſtill more remarkable object than it would otherwiſe have been. Similar tables were ſet before the reſt of the company. While we were taking our collation, wreſtlers, muſicians, and jugglers were buſied in their ridiculous performances, to which we did not deign to pay the ſmalleſt attention, although the old Emperor was ſo much amuſed with them, that he ordered money to be diſtributed to theſe buffoons as a proof of his approbation.

At ſun-ſet the fire-works began, which were almoſt ſimilar to the laſt, and terminated likewiſe
by

by a sham fight, which was perfectly well executed. The leaders of the court, who were stationed in the upper story, had also the pleasure of partaking of this festival.

The fire-works being over, his Imperial Majesty repaired to a habitation in another part of this delightful retreat, going in a sled over the ice. We followed him in a flat sled, passing under trees, along a noble serpentine canal. We alighted at a great distance from our point of departure, and proceeded on foot to an illuminated edifice, near which the Emperor was already seated. We were desired to sit down on cushions upon the ground.

Some players began an insipid piece of buffoonery, after some singers had chaunted verses, the subject of which seemed to me to be the praises of his Majesty, celebrated and honoured by all the nations of the earth; for I remarked that mention was made of the Dutch.

Having remained half an hour longer in this place, the Monarch retired. We were then reconducted to the canal, where we got into a sled, which conveyed us, by a circuitous route, to a gate, where we found our carts. There the

Naa-fan-tayen, who had alfo accompanied us the whole of this evening, took leave of us. We ftepped into our carriages to return to the city, and congratulated ourfelves when we got back to our lodgings, at paft nine o'clock, fo tirefome and difagreeable had been the conftant jolting of our vehicles.

The only recompenfe for the fatigue we fuffered in this fhort journey was the fight we obtained of the above-mentioned noble canal, forming feveral meanders through a wood in uneven ground. Its banks are compofed of rocks, which, being ufed inftead of bricks or ftones, have taken, under the hand of man, a form which they feem only to have received from that of nature. How great muft be the pleafure of navigating, in the fummer feafon, on this tranquil ftream in a light yacht, under the pleafant fhade of trees, which at this moment only exift to afflict the eye!

How happy were we to have feen this part of the Emperor's country feat, which to this day had remained unknown to us! Perhaps, indeed, we have not feen the twentieth part of the beauties contained in *Yuen-ming-yuen*; for I have been affured that its total circumference is little fhort of three hundred *li* (thirty leagues).

We remained in our hotel, whither our court conductor came to defire us to hold ourfelves in readinefs to go at feven o'clock to-morrow morning to the palace, where we are to receive the Emperor's letter for our Prince, and the laft prefents, becaufe it is only then that our audience of leave will really take place.

Our correfpondence with the Miffionaries is now entirely open, by means of our Chinefe domeftics. We accordingly communicate with them daily; but we cannot indulge ourfelves in the effufions, nor feel the pleafure refulting from the prefence of thofe whom we are happy to fee. We have reafon, neverthelefs, to be thankful for this imperfect enjoyment.

10th. Although ready to fet off at a very early hour, we were not conducted to court till eleven o'clock. We paffed an hour in one of the apartments of the weft fide, over the inner court, into which the fouth gate leads. The *Naa-fan-tayen* joined us there, and took us to an outer court, through the fouth gate, at a fmall diftance from which we were drawn up in a line. There the *Liepou-chong-tfu*, or Chief of the Tribunal of Ceremonies, an aged man, who wore an hexagonal oval button of a purple colour, came

to

to congratulate his Excellency and me on our being about to receive the laſt mark of the Emperor's favour.

We then performed, in obedience to the regular word of command given by a Mandarin in the train of the *Licpou*, the ceremony of proſtration in honour of the Emperor, after which the laſt preſents of the Emperor were delivered to us, confiſting of the following articles:

For the Prince of Orange—Eighty rolls of filk, and two ſmall vaſes of the ſtone called *yu-chi*.
For the Ambaſſador—Thirty-four rolls of filk, and a hundred and fifty *taels* of fine filver.
For me—Eight rolls of filk, and eighty *taels* of filver.
For the five gentlemen in the ſuite of the Embaſſy—Eight rolls of filk, and forty *taels* of filver each.
For the Mechaniſt, and the ſeventeen ſoldiers and ſervants—Four ſmall rolls of *panche* (plain narrow filk) and fifteen *taels* of filver each.

Our ſalute of honour, by way of thankſgiving, having terminated the ceremony, we returned by the weſt gate, where we found our little carts waiting in the outer court: we conſequently paſſed along the outſide of the palace-walls.

The

The Emperor's letter for our Prince has not yet been delivered to us, becaufe it is not yet ready; but it will be fent to us to-morrow, or the day after.

In the afternoon, the *Naa-fan-tayen* came to fpeak to us on bufinefs, and particularly to enquire what letters and effects we had brought for the Miffionaries. We gave him exact information on both thofe points.

I took this opportunity to repeat my requeft to fee my friend Grammont, as alfo for permiffion to go and examine the great bell. The *Naa-fan-tayen* affured us that he would ufe his beft endeavours with the *Voo-tchong-tang*; and when going away flattered us with hopes of feeing, at leaft, two of the Miffionaries before our departure from *Pe-king*.

The prefents intended for the two principal Minifters, and the *Naa-fan-tayen*, were ftill in our poffeffion. To-day, however, a kind of arrangement has been made for the acceptance of the principal articles, on condition of our taking a few trifles in return, in order to give the appearance of an exchange to this gift, which would be contrary to the Emperor's prohibition,

forbidding

forbidding all the Mandarins to accept prefents, under the penalties of forfeiting their employs and dignities. This affair was fettled with the *Naa-fan-tayen* to the fatisfaction of both parties.

11th. The Mandarins of Canton came to concert meafures with us for our journey. They took charge of the Emperor's prefents to the Stadtholder, in order to have them carefully packed up, and to deliver them to us at Canton.

Our court conductor affured us, that his Majefty, while giving an audience of leave to the firft of our Canton conductors, ordered him exprefsly to let us travel as might beft fuit our convenience, and with all the accommodations it might be poffible to procure; to take care that a good reception be given us on our route, and that honours be paid us in the principal cities, fuitable to the title of Ambaffador; to let us fee every thing curious, &c. &c. We may then hope that our journey back will be agreeable, efpecially, as among the Chinefe, an Ambaffador, or even a private individual, who has been admitted into the prefence of the Emperor, always enjoys much more confideration than before. We have then more than one reafon to think we fhall be better treated, at the fame time that
there

there will be no motive for accelerating our journey, its lasting a week or two, more or less, being a thing of no importance.

12th. The Prime Minister sent a Mandarin to take the letters addressed to the Missionaries. M. de Guignes, who was the depositary of them, hesitated at first to deliver them; but fearing lest the refusal might produce something unpleasant, he at last determined to give up all the packets, which were immediately carried to the palace, where we were assured the Missionaries were then waiting to receive them.

I again asked whether I should be permitted to see M. Grammont, and was told I should; but I am much afraid that there is a determination to prevent our seeing any Missionary. The Mandarins, from the highest to the lowest, must certainly be conscious of great culpability, or they would not think it necessary to carry distrust to such a length. It is easy also to see how great is the influence exercised by the regency of Canton over the first personages in the empire, since it even goes to the prevention of a communication between the Missionaries and us, which could not, however, be attended with any ill consequences.

13th. We

13th. We have been very bufy in packing up our baggage, which will be fent off to-morrow, in order that by its being continually before us, we may never be obliged to wait for any thing.

I muft mention here, as fomething extraordinary, that we have again ate this day of the fturgeon which his Majefty made us a prefent of on the 11th of January, the day after our arrival here. The froft has kept it perfectly fweet, without there having been occafion to employ a fingle grain of falt. We even expect to carry fome away, to ferve us on the road; but that portion we fhall falt.

14th. Towards noon, M. Roux, a French Miffionary, was introduced with a train of at leaft a dozen Mandarins of different claffes. They came to receive the cafes of wine, and other things that we had brought for the different Miffionaries, as well as what we ourfelves intended for Monfieurs Roux and Grammont. We were permitted to have half an hour's converfation with him, during which time every eye was upon the watch, to fee that we put no paper into his hand, and that we communicated nothing to him on the part of any one elfe.

This converfation was, however, a matter of fupererogation; for during feveral days/ paſt we had, by means of our fervants, conveyed backward and forward every thing that by reafon of its fmall bulk could be fubtracted from the inquifition of the Chinefe. Befides, the refidence of the French Miffionaries being only on the other fide of the handfome bridge, which ftands in our neighbourhood, our native fervants went there daily with our letters, and brought back the anfwers.

The nature of M. Roux's vifit convinced us ftill more ftrongly of the diftruft with which we have infpired the Chinefe. It ferves alfo to make our departure more defirable, efpecially as we were informed by M. Roux, that M. Grammont had in vain folicited permiffion of the Prime Minifter to join him in his vifit. Being thus affured that there is no difpofition to let us fee any thing more, either the great bell, or the temples, in regard to which I had expreffed fome curiofity, we look forward to the day of our leaving *Pe-king* with pleafure.

After M. Roux had paffed a full half-hour with us, the Mandarins began to prefs him to take the things he came for, and to retire with them. He

He was confequently obliged to leave us, though with great regret.

In the afternoon the Emperor's letter to the Stadtholder was at laft brought. It was put upon a table in the great court-yard of the hotel, whither his Excellency and I went to perform the falute of honour. The letter was afterwards taken out of its bamboo cafe, and fhewn to us. The whole is upon one page of a large fheet of coloured and fhining Chinefe paper, and is written in the Tartarian, Chinefe, and Latin languages. A lift was added to it of the prefents made by the Emperor to the Prince, as well as of thofe which he has beftowed upon each individual of the Embaffy. The Ambaffador read the Latin letter and thought it very fingular. As foon as he had done, the letter, enclofed in its yellow cover, was put into its cafe, and then a Mandarin took charge of it, in order to deliver it to us at Canton.

Shortly after this ceremony, our baggage was begun to be put into carts until night came, and interrupted the bufinefs. I obferved that thefe carriages have alfo bar-wheels, inftead of fpokes, and a fixed axle round which the wheel turns. In that refpect alone they differ from thofe I defcribed

fcribed on the 4th of January. They refemble them in every thing elfe, even to the harnefs.

Before I take leave of *Pe-king*, I think it incumbent on me to make a few obfervations on the ufual conftruction of the Chinefe houfes in the north of the empire, as well as on the manner in which the Chinefe warm their apartments.

In all China the houfes are built upon the ground; that is to fay, without having any cellar under them. The apartments are paved with flat fquare bricks, a thing very agreeable in warm weather, but very little fuitable to the fevere feafon of the year.

To defend them from the piercing cold which they experience in the northern parts of the Empire, the Chinefe have devifed fubterraneous furnaces, placed outfide the houfes in excavations made on purpofe. Tubes go branching off from thefe furnaces in every direction, under the bricks of the floors, and under a kind of platforms or eftrades on which the Chinefe fleep. They even pafs through the walls, which divide the different rooms, fo that the heat diffufed by thefe tubes produces in the apartments the temperature defired. The fire is kept up night and day in the outer ſtove or furnace, without the ſmalleſt danger to the buildings, becauſe a coat of bricks cloſely confines that deſtructive element, and oppoſes its diſaſtrous effects. If the apartments be ſpacious and numerous, an increaſed number of ſtoves and tubes always inſure the ſame reſult.

It cannot be denied that this is an invention honourable to Chineſe induſtry; and certainly it is no ſmall advantage, in a ſevere climate, to enjoy in the midſt of winter's cold an agreeable heat diffuſed through all the apartments. It is in thoſe places eſpecially, where theſe outer ſtoves are wanting, and where there is a neceſſity of having recourſe to the braſiers of charcoal of which I have ſpoken elſewhere, that the value of this invention is the moſt ſenſibly felt.

The *Naa-ſan-tayen* came early in the evening to take leave of us, and wiſh us a pleaſant journey. He renewed his aſſurance that he would recommend me particularly to the *Tſong-tou*, and the *Hou-pou* of Canton, and that his letters ſhould precede our arrival there. He alſo ſaid again, that perhaps he ſhould be *Hou-pou* there himſelf the enſuing year, and that in that caſe he would afford ſpecial protection to the Dutch nation, with whoſe agents he ſhould be happy to form a
friendly

friendly connection. He took leave of us with remarkable affability, and with demonstrations of kindnefs which befpoke the confummate courtier. I attended him as far as the door of the ftreet.

I have fince learnt that from our hotel he went to examine one of the two pieces of mechanifm, which is entirely repaired and put to rights by M. Petit Pierre; that he found the workmanfhip and the contrivance equally excellent. He expreffed great fatisfaction at òne of thefe pieces being mended, becaufe it would afford the means of judging of the merit and value of our prefents.

M. Roux went alfo to infpect the fame piece of mechanifm in the afternoon, which gave the five gentlemen, whom curiofity had carried there, likewife an opportunity to converfe for two hours with the Miffionary. He was much ftruck with the beauty of the piece in queftion, and related that at the time of the delivery of our prefents to the Emperor two very common things of the fame kind, brought from Canton, had been put in the place of ours, by way of avoiding the neceffity of telling his Majefty that they had been damaged on the road. He affirmed befides that it was the plan of the Mandarins to get the Prime Minifter to prefent ours to the Emperor on fome folemn occafion, without faying a word of their coming from the Dutch. The Mandarin, who was charged with the conveyance of the baggage from Canton, was indeed fharply reprimanded for his negligence by the Prime Minifter; but the excufe was, that all the blame was attributable to the bad package of our mechanift. By thefe means they deceive the Emperor, in whofe name the *Voo-tchong-tang* may be faid to govern and direct every thing as he pleafes.

We alfo learned from M. Roux that it is very probable that if the Embaffy had come directly from Europe or Batavia, we fhould have been permitted to communicate freely with the Miffionaries; but that, as we were all perfons refident at Canton except the Ambaffador, a mifplaced policy had made the Mandarins refufe us that favour.

The fame reafon was particularly powerful in regard to M. Grammont, who was near three years at Canton, where I had concerns with him, which increafed the apprehenfions of the Mandarins. There is really fomething bordering upon ftupidity in their fears. Is it not inconceivable that they have not been ftruck with the truth of the

the obfervation I made to one of them fome time fince; that having daily opportunities of making reprefentations to the Emperor and Prime Minifter, we fhould never think of recurring to Miffionaries, with whofe want of power we were but too well acquainted, fuppofing that we had any intentions of that kind, or any important thing to fay.

We have had the pleafure of M. Roux's company a great part of the morning. I afked him for information concerning the European buildings in the Imperial country-houfe of *Yuen-ming-yuen*. He told us that the plan of them had been defigned by Father Benoit, a French Miffionary in quality of architect; and that they had been built under his direction. The drawings which I have of them are very exact, having been copied from engravings made by the Miffionaries themfelves after the plans of their fellow-prieft.

M. Roux added, that the country-houfe of *Yuen-ming-yuen* contains thirty-fix diftinct habitations within its walls, at fome diftance from one another; that each of them has its dependencies, and the neceffary accommodations for the Emperor and his fuite, and that the European edifices

edifices form one of thirty-fix dwellings or divifions.

According to this account, of the authenticity of which I have not the fmalleft doubt, I have reafon to believe that we have not feen the twentieth part of the beauties of this immenfe domain, to which no habitation of any Prince in Europe is comparable, and of which the coft muft have amounted to a prodigious fum.

Our mechanift this day delivered the piece of mechanifm entirely repaired into the hands of a Mandarin, and of M. Roux, whom he apprifed of its conftruction, in order that the Chinefe may not fpoil it, as they were very near doing yefterday and to-day, by touching it while M. Petit Pierre was abfent.

15th. Our baggage being all upon the carts, we parted with M. Roux with great regret, and quitted our hotel. The Ambaffador and I took our carts as far as the gate of the city, where our palanquins were waiting for us. The gentlemen in the fuite of the Embaffy followed us on horfeback.

It was half paſt three in the afternoon when we ſet off. As ſoon as we were without the gate of the palace walls, our driver turned down a ſtreet leading to the ſouthward, keeping for ſome time cloſe to the rampart. Thence we proceeded to narrower and more irregular ſtreets, which took us a great way round, but at laſt brought us to the principal ſtreet adjoining to the gate called *Tchun-moun*, the very ſame by which we entered *Pe-king*, and which we now reached at twenty-five minutes after five.

In our way to the gate, I remarked on the eaſt ſide the church an obſervatory of the Portugueſe Miſſionaries, which overlook the houſes. The church is a handſome building, with a roof in the form of a croſs; and from a croſs ſtreet I perceived a very arched door of ſtone making the entrance of the edifice, the conſtruction of which is entirely European.

When I came to the ſuburbs of *Agauy-lautching*, outſide of the gate of *Tchun-moun*, and conſequently of the Tartarian city, my driver turned off in order to take a bye road, on one ſide of the main ſtreet, no doubt in order to avoid the crowd. This brought us to a little narrow ſtreet, and gave me an opportunity of convincing myſelf that the

F 4   lateral

lateral ſtreets are all very narrow, very irregular, and very different from the principal ones, which ſtand in the direction of the four cardinal points of the compaſs.

I alſo ſaw in the ſuburbs large ſpaces entirely open; gardens behind the houſes, and ſeveral places with mounts and rapid declivities, ſo that any one might have imagined himſelf in the midſt of the country. Hence I am of opinion that theſe ſuburbs are not regularly built upon, unleſs in the ſtreets which correſpond with the gates of the city, all the intermediate parts being probably as naked as the ſpace we paſſed through. I was very much ſurpriſed at it, for I ſuppoſed that ſuburbs, adjoining the Imperial reſidence, were entirely inhabited.

At half paſt four, we paſſed through the gate of the firſt city (the Chineſe town): this gate is ſituated to the weſtward, and is called the gate of *Tſay-ping*. When we came to the paved road, which I mentioned at the time of our arrival at *Pe-king*, and were at about five minutes walk from the above gate, we found our palanquins waiting for us. We bade an eternal adieu to our elegant carriages, in order to get into thoſe truly commodious vehicles, and continued our route over

the

the pavement. The road is not perfectly straight, taking several turns more or less perceptible; but its principal direction is east-south-east, and west-south-west. It keeps it as far as the little city of *Fee-ching-fé*, where after we had passed the handsome stone bridge, we found the road turn off to the south-south-west. At seven o'clock we passed through that same town of *Fee-ching-fé*, and arrived an hour afterwards at *Chin-tcheou-tin*, a village of moderate size, where we stopped at a paltry inn, being under the necessity of passing the night there, as the late hour of our departure had made it impossible for us to reach the lodging prepared for us thirty *li* farther off.

Our supper was very indifferent. Not having my bed, I was obliged to lie down upon the floor—a very bad specimen of our journey back.

16th. We proceeded on our journey at half past seven this morning, and at three o'clock reached *Lian-hiang-chen*, where we ought to have arrived yesterday evening.

I saw on the road three elegant temples, with convents, one of which is a spacious building.
All

All of them are inclofed with walls in the form of ramparts, kept in excellent repair.

We fet off at half paft eleven, and after being three hours upon the road ftopped at *Tan-tfin-y*, in order that our *Coulis* might take a repaft. We then fet off again, and at fix o'clock reached the fuburbs of *Tfo-tchou*, where tolerably good lodgings were prepared for us. In this part of our journey we faw four temples and convents of very neat appearance, one of which belongs to the fect of *Lamas*.

We alfo paffed over the magnificent bridge which I mentioned on the 8th of January. Here, however, I muft add, that at each extremity of it are large and handfome triumphal arches of wood with three paffages, and having each an open hexagonal pavilion at its fide. In thefe pavilions ftand feveral large ftones, bearing infcriptions in honour of the architect of the bridge, in the middle of which, and upon the north fide is a dome of yellow varnifhed tiles, alfo covering a monumental ftone. In front of the northern triumphal arch is another dome fupported by four rows of ftone pillars, each row confifting of four. On each fide of the

north

north entrance of this place there ftands on a ftone pedeftal an enormous lion of caft iron, painted of a greenifh colour to imitate that of bronze.

During our afternoon's journey we were overtaken at three o'clock by a violent north wind, which raifed clouds of duft fo thick as to intercept the light of the fun. It was impoffible to diftinguifh objects at twenty yards diftance, and we were almoft ftifled in our palanquins. The fury of the wind foon abated a little, but all the reft of the night bore, neverthelefs, a ftrong refemblance to a tempeft. We found on a wall in one of the apartments of our inn a Malay infcription, written in Arabic characters, of which M. de Guignes took a copy on account of its fingularity.

After a tolerable fupper we paffed a pretty good night.

17th. Having only fixty *li* to travel to-day, we did not fet off till a quarter paft nine. I remarked in the north-eaft part of the city two lofty towers ftanding clofe to each other, and exactly of the fame kind. In twenty-five minutes we went from one end of the town to the other in a right line from north to south. Beyond the south gate are suburbs of considerable extent.

To the east of the road is a large and handsome temple standing by a convent. In the walls common to both of them are three gates fronting the south, the middle one having three passages and being of enormous size. The front of these gates is a large square court, the sides of which are regularly planted with lofty trees, such as are not unfrequently seen round buildings of this sort.

A little further to the south we saw another temple, and a convent belonging to the *Lamas*, but less considerable in extent.

At half past eleven we came to another temple and another convent. The same thing occurred again at noon at the entrance of the village of *Faukoun*, where we halted half an hour to give our *Coulis* time to eat. Setting off afterwards we arrived at half past three at our lodgings without the walls of the little city of *Sin-ching-chen*, which were in the same public building where we were on the seventh of January at noon, and where we met with tolerable accommodations.

By

By making further enquiry we found that the building in which we are lodged is a pagoda dedicated to Saint *Itching-cong*, who inhabits the front hall. We were very well treated here, and enjoyed a good fupper and refrefhing fleep.

The weather was very cold to-day, the wind blowing ftrong from the fouth-weft, which again raifed fuffocating clouds of duft.

At a fmall diftance north of the city, I obferved in my way a tower conftructed like that which I had feen on the 9th of January near the city of *Pe-king*; that is to fay, that its lower part confifts only of one ftory, while the upper confifts of nine fmall ones, above which is a roof ending in a point.

Oppofite our lodgings, and to the weftward of a little river at prefent frozen, is a very handfome and very fpacious town-houfe, with a garden belonging to it. In the front of the building is a large piece of ground, overfhadowed on every fide by lofty trees, which feems to be a place of exercife for the troops. The edifice and the garden are inclofed behind and on the fides by a wall; but the efplanade is only protected

protected by a ditch or canal, with two bridges oppofite the building.

During our fhort ftay this morning in the village of *Fan-koun*, I had an opportunity of feeing a tinker execute what I believe is unknown in Europe. He mended and foldered frying-pans of caft iron that were cracked and full of holes, and reftored them to their primitive ftate, fo that they became as ferviceable as ever. He even took fo little pains to effect this, and fucceeded fo fpeedily as to excite my aftonifhment. It muft indeed appear impoffible to any one who has not been witnefs to the procefs.

All the apparatus of the workman confifts in a little box fixteen inches long, fix inches wide, and eighteen inches in depth, divided into two parts. The upper contains three drawers, with the neceffary ingredients; in the lower is a bellows, which, when a fire is wanted, is adapted to a furnace eight inches long and four inches wide. The crucibles for melting the fmall pieces of iron intended to ferve as folder are a little larger than the bowl of a common tobacco pipe, and of the fame earth of which they are made in Europe; thus the whole bufinefs of foldering is executed.

The workman receives the melted matter out of the crucible upon a piece of wet paper, approaches it to one of the holes or cracks in the frying-pan, and applies it there, while his affiftant fmooths it over by fcraping the furface, and afterwards rubs it with a bit of wet linen. The number of crucibles which have been deemed neceffary are thus fucceffively emptied in order to ftop up all the holes with the melted iron, which confolidates and incorporates itfelf with the broken utenfil, and which becomes as good as new.

The furnace which I faw was calculated to contain eight crucibles at a time, and while the fufion was going on was covered with a ftone by way of increafing the intenfity of the heat.

18th. Setting off this morning at nine o'clock, we reached at twelve the little city of *Pay-kau-fe*, where the *Coulis* ftopped to refrefh. Proceeding on our journey we came at three o'clock to *Hiong-chen*, where we paffed the night in a very indifferent *Conquan*.

During the greateft part of the evening our road lay along the banks of a river, which was ftill blocked up by the ice. We went ten *li* towards

towards the south, thirty *li* to the south-south-east, and then twenty *li* in a south-east direction. The wind, which was at north-west for a short time, blew with much violence, and incommoded us as well with dust as with the cold.

This evening our second conductor solicited us very earnestly to consent to travel one hundred and twenty *li* to-morrow, in order to arrive at an early hour at the city of *Ho-kin-fou*, where we are to receive an entertainment and some presents on the part of the Emperor. The Ambassador, after a little hesitation, acquiesced.

19th. We were on our way this morning at half past six. At nine o'clock the *Coulis* took their breakfast at *Tchou-pé-hau*, and at half past twelve we reached the city of *Yin-kion-chen*, without the walls of which we stopped for half an hour in a public-house, in order to take some refreshment. Having accomplished our purpose we set off again, and at a quarter past five came to the town of *Y ii-pou*, where we passed the night very commodiously.

Our road, during the whole of this day, lay through a marshy country, and at some distance I perceived three or four lakes, which had been

concealed

concealed from me by the darknefs of the night when on my way to *Pe-king*.

I obferved, near the city of *Yin-kion-chen*, three tombs, having each a triumphal arch of ftone at their entrance; in the reft of the fpace between the gate and the grave ftand in fucceffion, and facing each other, two ftone pillars, two fitting lions, two rams lying down, two horfes faddled, and two ftatues of Mandarins. A little further on is a tomb overfhadowed by a thick grove of cyprefs.

At the entrance of *Chek-moun-kiou* we met with a monument compofed of a folid block of white marble, about ten feet high by two feet and a half wide, and one foot thick, ftanding upon the back of a tortoife, alfo cut out of a fingle ftone. An infcription is engraved upon the block.

Thefe are the only things that had efcaped me in going to *Pe-king*.

This morning our route was fouth, and then fouth-fouth-weft till about noon, when it refumed its firft direction. The wind, which was wefterly and blew very cold, abated in the afternoon.

20th. At

20th. At half paſt ſeven we quitted our lodging, and at a quarter paſt nine found ourſelves in the city of *Ho-kien-fou*, where we were firſt conducted to a public edifice to get our breakfaſt.

At half paſt eleven we were taken to the Imperial court, a building conſtructed in all the capital cities of provinces, and even in ſome others that are not dignified with that title. The Emperor's tablet (*chap*) which is placed upon an altar in the principal hall, receives the ſalute of honour at every new and full moon from all the Mandarins. A diſcharge of artillery and military muſic announced our paſſage; firſt, before the troops that were drawn up in a line, and then in front of a long file of Mandarins. After theſe was the Governor of the Province and another great Mandarin who congratulated his Excellency and me on our arrival, and who conducted us to an outer hall to ſhew us the Emperor's preſents and entertainment, and then to the great hall beyond it. There, with the two great Mandarins and our two firſt conductors, we performed the ſalute before the Emperor's *chap* with our heads covered. We then returned to the outer hall, where we were deſired defired to fit down upon cufhions, by little tables covered with fweetmeats and paftry.

As foon as we were feated a company of comedians began to perform upon a very neat theatre, erected on purpofe oppofite the hall. Several hot difhes, particularly roaft and boiled meat, were afterwards ferved up, and cups of *Samfou* were prefented to us for our beverage. We were waited upon by Mandarins of the gold button. We tafted a variety of things, and after having remained till nearly half paft twelve, we rofe, took leave, and departed.

The prefents confifted of four half rolls of filk, and four pieces of narrow flowered filk (*pelang*) for the Ambaffador, and the fame for me. Half as much of the fame articles was given to each of the five gentlemen in the fuite of the Embaffy, and the reft of his retinue received a few pieces of plain *panche*. The whole of thefe gifts were put into a little box, of which one of the Mandarins took charge.

We paffed through a very long ftreet, lined on both fides with temporary fhops, full of all forts of merchandize, and having much refemblance

blance to an European fair. The city is very populous, although we perceived fo many fpots not built upon, that we had reafon to think that fcarcely a fourth of the fpace inclofed by the walls is occupied. And even in the part that is, a great many houfes are in a ruinous condition, as I had before occafion to obferve.

The two gates of the city through which we paffed are both guarded externally by a femicircular baftion, having two lateral entrances. This mode of conftruction is common to all the baftions that ftand before the gates of the Chinefe cities, fo that the openings of the baftions and the gates of the town can never be enfiladed upon the fame line. In the middle of thefe baftions four fmall iron guns are placed upon a heap of ftones, with their muzzles turned towards the paffage, and in this confifts the whole of their defence, which we could not help confidering as highly ridiculous.

Our road conducted us through feveral villages and hamlets. We alfo faw feveral pagodas in fo ruinous a ftate that idols, which no doubt in former days were the objects of great veneration, were now expofed to the injuries of the air.

We

We arrived at a quarter paſt five at the city of *Hien-chen*, where lodgings for the night had been prepared for us with ſome degree of care. We found the ramparts of this place in ſtill worſe condition than when we paſſed through it before, and the houſes make no better an appearance than thoſe of the moſt miſerable hamlet.

In theſe parts the farmers are already very buſy in carrying manure upon the land intended for feed. In another place, and towards the afternoon I ſaw ground ſown by means of a machine of very ſimple conſtruction.

It conſiſts of two ſticks or pieces of wood about four feet long, the lower extremities of which are ſhod with a kind of iron wedge that ſerves to open the furrow. A little above is a ſquare box placed between the two ſticks, and tapering downwards in the ſhape of a funnel. Behind this is a plank put acroſs for the purpoſe of covering up the furrow after the feed has fallen in. This inſtrument is put in motion by means of two wheels. Two Chineſe draw it, while a third who guides with his two hands, firſt ſows one, and then the other furrow. I had already conceived from the regularity with which I obſerved every thing growing in the fields that ſome ma-

G 3   chine

chine was employed for fowing, and I was not a little pleafed at having an opportunity of feeing both the inftrument and the manner in which it is ufed.

-21ft. We fet off at eight o'clock with the intention of travelling eighty *li*. At nine we paffed by the little city of *Chin-ka-kien*, which is deftitute of ramparts, and the two gates of which are tumbling to ruins. Beyond the fouth gate is a ftone bridge which appears to have ftood for ages, but which is ftill in good condition. As yet I had not feen any of fo fingular a conftruction.

This bridge has four great femi-circular arches, and three fmaller ones placed at the top of the intervals between them, fo that the upper portion of the piers, which is in general a folid mafs, here affords an additional paffage upon an increafe of the river. The water at fuch times finds a way through the fupplementary arches as well as through the three principal ones, and as the action of the ftream is thus diminifhed, there is no longer any danger of the bridge being carried away. I could not help praifing this provident invention, and admiring the genius who conceived

ceived the idea and the utility refulting from its fuccefs.

At a quàrter paft eleven we arrived at *Fau-ching-ek*, another little city alfo without ramparts, but not without gates. We there made a fcanty dinner; and fetting off again at half paft twelve arrived at a quarter paft three in the fuburbs of the city of *Fau-ching-chen*, where we paffed a comfortable night.

From *Pe-king* hither all the crows we had met with were entirely black. However this afternoon I faw two with the upper part of their necks white. I had already been furprifed in going towards the capital of China, at my never having feen any black crows in the fouthern provinces, and at not feeing any pied ones in the north.

Arriving at an early hour at *Fau-ching-chen*, I fent one of the fervants of the Mandarins in fearch of fuch a fowing machine as I had feen yefterday. He brought me one immediately, but it was double, that is to fay, fo contrived as to fow two furrows at a time. I paid a dollar and a half for it, and mean to take it with me. It is, however, very different from that defcribed above,

above, having no wheels, and being of a more complicated conſtruction. This acquiſition gives me a great deal of pleaſure.

We ſet off at half paſt ſeven, and a little after eleven reached the ſuburbs of *King-tcheou*, where we made a very haſty dinner.

This city is remarkable for a very lofty octagonal tower of twelve ſtories, that I had not ſeen on my way to *Pe-king* by reaſon of the night. We paſſed through a ſtreet, in which ſtand three very handſome triumphal arches of ſtone. *King-tcheou* may alſo boaſt of ramparts kept in very good repair, and of a very lofty temple of three ſtories at a ſmall diſtance from the tower. The houſes are very mean, outſide at leaſt; for in China there is no judging of the inſide, the handſomeſt palace ſeldom exhibiting any thing but four dead walls, except indeed the gate-way in the front. It is the ſame with regard to the houſes, unleſs they be ſhops, in which caſe they are open to the ſtreet.

Setting off again at half paſt twelve, we reached in two hours the territory of the province of *Chan-tong*, in which the ſoldiers drew up in
front

front of all the guard-houses upon the road as we were paffing by.

I obferved with aftonifhment in the province of *Tché-li*, where there are guard-houfes at five *li* diftance from one another, that they are almoft all in bad condition, and many of them abfolutely tumbling down. It feldom happened that we faw fo many as three or four foldiers come out of them, which furprifed me the more, as it was natural to think that in the province of which the Emperor makes his refidence things would be better regulated than elfewhere. Here, however, the very contrary is the cafe.

The period of our days journey was *Tétcheou*, where to-morrow we are to partake of an entertainment, and to receive prefents on the part of his Imperial Majefty. A quarter of an hour before we arrived there we met with two triumphal arches. In the fpace intervening between them the road was lined with the garrifon of the city, through the ranks of which we paffed in our palanquins, and at each triumphal arch were faluted with three guns. The fame was repeated when we came to the gates of the city. After having paffed through feveral ftreets we came to our lodgings, which confift of two buildings contiguous

tiguous to each other, and are confequently both fpacious and convenient.

The city is not large, but is furrounded by a ftrong wall. It appears to contain a number of good houfes, as far at leaft as we could judge from their exterior. Its population is alfo confiderable, but it can boaft of nothing worth the attention of the traveller.

A fhort time before we entered the city we paffed the river over a bridge of boats, and found its banks crowded with the fame veffels that were there when we were on our way to *Pe-king*. The ice is, however, broken up, but many portions of it are floating down the ftream.

Soon after our arrival at our lodgings the Governor of the city, a Mandarin of the blue tranfparent button, came to congratulate us on our return, and to enquire after our health. The fame thing was done by another great Mandarin, the next in dignity to the Governor.

This evening we were joined by our third conductor, who, by his kindnefs and attention fince our departure from *Pe-king*, has entirely recovered our good opinion, and even acquired

our

our friendſhip. He informed the Ambaſſador that there are from this town two roads, both of which lead to the place where we are to embark; one running along thoſe parts of the province of *Chan-tong*, through which we had paſſed in coming, and the other going right acroſs that province, and even ſaving us a whole days journey; he added that we might take the one moſt agreeable to his Excellency. For the ſake of variety, that which croſſes *Chan-tong* was preferred, and the diſtance regulated which we were to travel every day. The reſult is that our journey through that province will take up nine days. We ſhall then travel by land three days more in the province of *Kiang-nam*, as far as *Von-ka-ſen*, at a ſhort diſtance from which we ſhall find boats ready to receive us. Hence we promiſe ourſelves a great deal of pleaſure ariſing from a new country and new objects.

At half paſt nine o'clock this morning we were invited to go to the Imperial Court, ſituated at the angle of the ſouth-eaſt part of the city, near which, upon a ſharp-pointed baſtion, ſtand a pagoda and a ſmall tower. The latter is only four ſtories high, but the ſtile of the architecture is pleaſing.

We

We were received at the court with a repetition of the ceremonies performed at *Ho-kien-fou* on the 20th of this month. The hall and the theatre were here more ornamented than at the former place; but the filk and other decorations were of a more ordinary kind.

At the moment when we had advanced to the front of the altar, in order to perform the ceremony of proftration, a letter was read to us from the Emperor to the Governor of the Province, importing, according to the tranflation of our *Lingua*, that his Majefty being very well pleafed with the Dutch Embaffy, as well as with the conduct of the Ambaffador and thofe who accompanied him, and wifhing to give them ftill farther proofs of his fatisfaction, ordered the Governor of the Province of *Chan-tong* to entertain us in his name, to make us prefents, and to treat us with the greateft refpect.

When the whole was read we performed the falute of honour, keeping our hats on while paying the cuftomary compliments and civilities to the different Mandarins. We were then defired to fit down upon cufhions placed by the fide of fmall tables covered with paftry and fruit, which

were

were removed to make room for two succeffive courses of boiled meat and vegetables.

As soon as we were seated the amusements began with tumblers, who made several leaps with remarkable addrefs.

The Imperial presents were precisely the same both in nature and quality as those of *Hau-kien-fou*; and here also were given in charge to our Mandarins.

We rose from table at half past ten, and took leave of the Mandarins, after thanking them for the handsome reception they had given us. We then seated ourselves once more in our palanquins. On quitting the suburbs we were paid the same military honours as yesterday.

We proceeded along a small and wide road, which for the most part lay between fields of arable land of a better quality than that of the Province of *Tché-li*. We passed through no less than eleven villages and hamlets, and discovered at least double that number on the two sides of the road. At about half a league from the city of *Ping-yuen-chen*, is a noble hexagonal tower of seven stories, with projecting roofs at each. It

stands

ſtands in the midſt of the fields, and is entirely inſulated.

Still nearer the town is a tomb with a triumphal arch of ſtone, and figures ſimilar to thoſe that I deſcribed under the date of the 19th of this month; except that here two elephants ſtood next to the horſes. The city is announced by delightful environs; trees of various kinds and magnitude; hamlets interſperſed with groves of cedar and cypreſs, covering with their ſhade the laſt aſylum of man: every thing concurred to render the proſpect one of the moſt intereſting that I had ſeen for a long time; particularly when gilded by the rays of the ſetting ſun.

We have this day ſeen a greater number of orchards than in any other part of our journey.

On coming to the city of *Ping-yuen-chen*, we found the garriſon under arms, and were ſaluted while paſſing by. When we reached the gate, we were conducted through the principal ſtreet, where formerly ſtood five triumphal arches of ſtone, of four of which no more than the pedeſtal and a few fragments now remain. From thence we were taken to the vicinity of the ſouth gate, where we found excellent accommodations and

and a good table in a very large building, opposite the door of which stands another magnificent triumphal arch of stone.

The Regent or Governor of the city came to pay his compliments to us, and made an apology for not treating us better. We replied to his courtesy in suitable terms, and he retired after a short conversation.

This city, which forms a long square, is surrounded with handsome walls, but not more than one half of its internal space is built upon. To the westward are several edifices in tolerably good condition, in the number of which we remarked a very neat temple covered with green varnished tiles. It was by ascending to the top of the rampart and of the gate of the city, by means of a flight of brick steps, that I was enabled to discern those objects.

At the entrance of a narrow street near our lodgings is a triumphal arch of stone, similar to that which stands in front of our present abode, and which proves that it was once the residence of some distinguished persons, whose virtues have been deemed worthy of celebration.

In

In our very lodgings one of the halls contains feveral coffins inclofing dead bodies. Several of them bear marks of great antiquity, and yet they are ftill preferved. This is indeed a favourite cuftom among the Chinefe of very elevated rank.

I was once in a pagoda at Honam, oppofite Canton, in which coffins are likewife depofited in little rooms or feparate fpaces, and was affured that fome of them were more than a century old.

There is a particular fpecies of wood in China confidered as unperifhable; of this they make coffins, fome of which coft more than a hundred and fifty Louis d'ors. The Chinefe, let his pecuniary means be ever fo fmall, procures while living, either for himfelf or his family, the beft wood he can buy, and keeps it with great care at the entrance of his houfe till wanted for the laft abode of a being who is no more, but whofe pride has furvived him.

23d. Almoft the whole of this day our road took a fouth-eaft direction, and at a quarter paft five in the evening we had travelled more than eighty *li* (eight leagues). We were carried by a body of *Coulis*, who have been with us ever fince the seventeenth,

seventeenth, and whom we shall probably retain till we come to the place where we are to take water. The consequence is that we can now proceed on our journey, and stop where we please, without suffering the inconveniences, and even the torments that were so liberally dispensed to us by those wretches in our way to *Pe-king*.

It is surprising however that the *Coulis* are able to undergo such fatigue. Each palanquin has three relays, or twelve bearers, and a guide. Four *Coulis* carry the palanquin for half an hour, while two others walk by the side of it. They have, it is true, a cart in which six men may sit and rest themselves; but one half of them are always actively employed.

This evening a visit was paid us by two provincial Mandarins, who both wear the dark blue button, and who are to accompany us as long as within their district. One of them is, however, of more elevated dignity than the other; the covering of his palanquin being of an olive green, and his train consisting of no less than twenty-seven persons on horseback. These two Mandarins passed about an hour with us. They smoaked a pipe, drank a glass of Cape wine, and then left us, us, apparently well satisfied with the reception we had given them.

24th. We set off this morning at seven o'clock, and were saluted as we passed, both at the south and east gate. It was by the latter that we left the city, and at the extremity of the suburbs we were received by fresh discharges of artillery and other military honours. During this day and yesterday we have not passed a single guard-house without the soldiers turning out, and drawing up in a line.

At a quarter past twelve we reached the town of *Un-chan-kiou*, where we dined. While we were approaching it, the whole garrison turned out under arms, with colours flying, and did the same at the other end of the place when we left it.

At a quarter past five we came to the town of *Tsi-hochen ousang*, the end of our day's journey, where we met with tolerable accommodations. This place makes a much better appearance outside than many cities, and is of considerable size. We have this day passed through, or close by, thirteen villages, and have perceived a still greater number at a small distance from the road.

This

This morning I had the curiofity to count the villages that I could fee from my palanquin without change of pofture, and found one and twenty in the fpace which my eye took in, and which might comprife about three fourths of the circle of the horizon. An hour after I began again, and a like number prefented themfelves to my view. Hence we may conclude that this part of the province is inhabited by more cultivators than the weftern diftricts, which we paffed through in our way to *Pe-king*, and which appeared to us fo wretchedly poor.

All the day we paffed between corn fields, which in the fummer feafon, when embellifhed by verdure, enamelled with flowers, and enriched with a yellow harveft, muft compofe a very delightful landfcape.

In the afternoon we paffed clofe to the city of *Yu-hing-chen*, which, from without, and from the fpot whence we had a view of it, appeared to be a pretty large place, furrounded with good ramparts. On the outfide of the eaft and fouth gates there are two magnificent temples, with other buildings belonging to them, ftanding within the fame walls. Their roofs are covered with

with green varnifhed tiles, and the whole is kept in very good repair.

25th. We proceeded on our journey at half paſt ſeven, and found the troops drawn up at the end of the town. At a quarter paſt nine we reached the city of *Tſi-ho-chen*, where we dined. The garriſon here was alſo under arms. The city is ſurrounded with handſome walls, is handſomely built, and appears very populous. In front of the north gate is an Imperial pavilion, in which ſtands a ſtone monument, and a little farther on, a great pagoda in very good preſervation.

In the interior of the city, near the ſouth gate, is alſo an Imperial pagoda, and a ſtone monument bearing an inſcription.

Setting off at half paſt ten we paſſed a river beyond the gate, over which ſtands a very ſolid ſtone bridge, two hundred and ſeventy-five paces long. We began now to approach the mountains, which we ſaw for the firſt time ſince our departure from *Pe-king*.

In the afternoon we paſſed to the weſtward of a temple and and an immenſe convent. To the
ſouth

south are three gates, with three paſſages leading through the centre one, and within the circuit of the walls ſtand no leſs than twenty buildings in very good repair. Before theſe gates is a large open ſquare ſpace, having on two ſides a conſiderable building ſurrounded with a double row of lofty trees, making altogether a very handſome appearance.

At half paſt one we entered into a deep valley between two mountains, very narrow at its entrance, and ſkirted on both ſides by ſteep rocks. We paſſed through five villages ſituated in this valley; and perceived to the weſtward a caſtle ſeated on the ſummit of one of the higheſt mountains.

To the eaſtward of the town of *Chang-tſin-chen-anſang*; and upon the top of a mountain of conſiderable elevation, planted with cypreſs trees, ſtands a magnificent temple, incloſed with walls, and offering a very pleaſing object to the eye.

Half an hour afterwards we again croſſed a river by a bridge perfectly horizontal, through which are thirty-ſeven narrow paſſages for the water. All the ſtones with which it is built are of conſiderable dimenſions, and are faſtened together

gether on every fide with iron clamps, a thing I never obferved elfewhere.

At a quarter paft four we came to the village of *Chang-haya*, where we paffed the night in a tolerable inn.

Our road for the moft part took a fouth-eaft direction. The wind which blew violently from the fouth, while we were paffing through the gorge of the mountains, raifed a duft which incommoded us a good deal.

Before we arrived at thofe mountains we had paffed, as on the preceding day, between fields of arable land, and had alfo met with a great number of villages.

We obferved to-day a great number of orchards, particularly in the neighbourhood of habitations. Pears, which were here very large, were fold by the road fide. Yefterday one was given me at my lodgings, which meafured fourteen inches round, and taken lengthwife fifteen and a half. This kind of pear appears to be the only one known in the northern provinces. Its colour is a beautiful fhining yellow. Before it it is pared it feems hard, but when eaten, it is juicy, melting, and of an agreeable tafte.

In Europe there are feveral forts I fhould prefer to this, although it is the beft I ever ate in China.

At *Pe-king* I never faw more than one fort of apple, which is of a very indifferent quality, mealy, of an infipid flavour, and more calculated to pleafe the eye than the tafte.

I remarked this morning in the city, while walking through the market-place, a confiderable quantity of yellow carrots, of very extraordinary length and thicknefs, fince they are much bigger than thofe of Hoorn in Holland. They appear to be very common. There were alfo turnips of prodigious fize, the fkin of which is of a crimfon-colour.

As to the houfes I was furprifed at their all having very lofty roofs covered with thatch or tiles, and not flat ones as in the weftern parts of the province of *Chan-tong*, and in that of *Tché-li*. I alfo obferved that none of the caftles fo frequently met with in the provinces I have juft mentioned are to be feen here.

Chang-haya,

Chang-haya, the village where we ſtopped is very extenſive and populous, and contains a number of ſhops of every kind. Its ſituation among the mountains gives it a very ſtriking appearance.

The road appeared to be much frequented, and in the courſe of the day we met with a number of wheel-barrows carrying confiderable loads. Favoured by a ſtrong gale they made a very advantageous uſe of their ſails, which as I had to-day an opportunity of obſerving, ſpare the barrow men a great deal of labour. This adjunct is then a thing of real utility.

26th. Setting off at ſeven o'clock in the morning we came in three hours after to the town of *Kong-chan-pu*, where we dined at a very good inn. Having ſtaid an hour and a half in this place we refumed our journey, and at half paſt three reached the ſuburb of *Tay-ngan-tcheou*, where we are to ſleep in very indifferent lodgings. Military honours were every where paid us.

We travelled to-day between mountains. Sometimes we were in a very level road, at others in a hollow or ſtony one, that took an eaſt

by

by south direction. We passed, at some distance, from two towns called *Kong-chan-chion*, and *Long-chin-chen*, besides eleven villages and other places of less note.

The mountains were barren and rocky; not the smallest verdure was to be seen on them. The level space between them is nevertheless cultivated as much as the nature of the soil will permit.

We also passed over several bridges, and saw several triumphal arches built of stone, and like them wearing the appearance of great antiquity.

We perceived that the temperature of the air was much milder, and the heat of the sun more powerful. At four in the afternoon Fahrenheit's thermometer stood at sixty one degrees.

27th. We left our *conquan* at eight o'clock in the morning, and were conducted along the rampart without the town, which is very large and exceedingly populous. Near the gate on the north side is a great and very handsome pagoda, which we had the curiosity to visit yesterday in our afternoon's walk.

At

At a quarter paſt eleven we arrived, by a very level road, at the town called *Chui-ku-chau.* We ſtopped there to dinner. It was the nineteenth place we had paſſed through or ſeen in the courſe of the morning. Setting out again at twelve o'clock we had all the afternoon a very uneven road, being obliged to paſs over the ſummit of four mountains, one of which was of very great elevation.

At a quarter paſt four we reached the town of *Yong-lau-chen,* the ſeventh place that had preſented itſelf to our view this afternoon. This night we put up at a very indifferent *conquan.* The town appeared pretty large and tolerably well inhabited on the north ſide. We ſaw a magnificent temple and a convent, both ſtanding within the ſame walls.

During the day our road has almoſt conſtantly taken a direction to the ſouth-eaſt by eaſt, and eaſt-ſouth-eaſt. Several fine proſpects produced by the different poſitions of the mountains which preſent to us a variety of diſtant views, eſpecially when we come to any riſing ground; the continuation of fair weather and a warmer climate; every thing in ſhort concurred to render our journey more agreeable and commodious. We could now

now travel with pleafure as much as a hundred or a hundred and twenty *li* (ten or twelve leagues) a day. The Mandarins, our conductors, do every thing in their power to oblige us, and till this moment we have not had the fmalleft occafion for complaint, which is equally fatisfactory to them and to us.

28th. Having a hundred and thirty *li* to go we fet off this morning at half paft fix. Traveling for the firft two hours along a handfome and ftraight road, and afterwards afcending feveral mountains, we came at a quarter paft ten to the fuburbs of *Sin-tay-chen*, where we were to dine.

We proceeded on our journey at half paft eleven, being carried along the ramparts of this little city, which are kept in very good repair. During the afternoon we were conftantly going up and down hill till a quarter paft four, when we paffed by the city of *Mong-in-chen*, where the road again became level and continued to be fo till half paft five, the time of our arrival at the town of *Kiang-cha-fin*. We ftaid there all the night, having travelled a hundred and forty *li* (fourteen leagues).

The

The city of *Mong-in-chen* is small, but it appears closely built. As the road passes along a mountain which commands it, we were able to see into the interior over the walls, which are solidly built and in good repair. In the centre of the town stands a large building two stories high, but the rest of the houses make a very indifferent appearance. The suburb contains as many houses as the town itself, and is full of shops.

Sin-tay-chen is also a small place, and the house where we alighted, though the largest in it, contains nothing remarkable.

In the space we travelled over the remainder of the day, there was a great deal of cultivated land, but fewer habitations than we had seen during the preceding ones. The inhabitants were every where busied in carrying manure on the ground.

The great quantity of millet that I saw in the markets in this province and that of Chili, and the general use made of it in most families, as I had occasion to observe in passing through the villages, make me imagine that this kind of grain, which does not require strong land, is here the general object of cultivation.

1st. March.

1ft. March. Some backwardnefs in the payment of the *Coulis* occafioned a delay of our departure till three quarters after eight. The Mandarins were defirous of difcharging them, but we refufed to confent to it, as we were very well ferved by them till the prefent moment.

At a quarter paft twelve we came to *Teu-chang-y*, a town of tolerable appearance. After having dined, we fet off again at half paft one on our way to the village of *Tfang-ti-tfi*, where after travelling a hundred *li*, we are obliged to put up for the night at a very forry inn. Our road lay partly over a plain, and in part over very uneven ground. The laft portion of the road paffed over the fummit of mountains of lefs elevation than thofe of yefterday. We could however diftinguifh the different chains of them to a very great diftance.

We faw to-day more habitations than yefterday, and the number of cattle appeared alfo greater. During the laft two or three days I have remarked feveral numerous flocks of fheep, goats, and hogs grazing in the fields.

Since we have taken the new road along which we are now travelling, I have had an opportunity

nity of observing that many women and several of the men are afflicted with large tumours in the neck, a thing which we had not seen elsewhere, and which seem to bespeak an endemical disease.

We have been going almost constantly towards the south-east. The weather was very cloudy in the morning and threatened rain; but in the afternoon a violent north wind cleared the sky, and favoured the wishes of a number of barrow men by swelling the sails of their terrestrial boats.

2d. Our departure this morning took place at half past six. Our road led us over mountains till nine o'clock, when we found ourselves at the foot of one of the most lofty of them, upon the summit of which stands a castle of considerable strength.

We had before passed over a stone bridge, with twenty-four narrow passages for the water; the stones of which it is constructed being connected with iron clamps in like manner as those of another bridge which I have already mentioned. The stream over which this bridge affords a passage is very small, this season being the dryest of the year.

A little

A little after ten o'clock we found ourselves on a level road, the mountains having left us, and about a quarter of an hour afterwards we arrived at the village of *Poun-chan*, where we dined and fet off again at half paft eleven. Before three o'clock we reached *Sin-chong-chen*, where we are to fleep, and where we are very well accommodated in a large building in the city.

A little before our arrival at the laft mentioned place, we met with a river of confiderable width. The town which is pretty large is furrounded by a good rampart. We have travelled to-day ninety *li*, in a fouth by eaft direction.

The country grows more populous; for this afternoon I counted from my palanquin twenty four different places. I faw with pleafure in the vicinity of all the habitations a great number of orchards, cultivated as in Europe.

This evening, the Mandarin who is our fecond conductor for the province of *Chan-tong*, came to take leave of us; becaufe as he finds himfelf approaching the limits of his province, it is his intention to return to-morrow. He told us that his companion had come to our lodgings yefterday with the fame intention, and finding us already gone, had fet off that fame day on his way home. We bade him adieu in the moft affectionate manner, wifhing him all manner of good fortune and rapid promotion. Born near *Hung-chau-chen*, in the province of *Quang-tong*, he entered into the Imperial corps of *Chiouais*, and upon leaving them, obtained the employ which he now holds. He appears defirous of permiffion to refign, in order that he may retire to his native place, where his mother refides.

The political fyftem of the Chinefe requires as a fundamental rule, that no Mandarin fhall ever be invefted with any authority in his native province. In confequence of this wife principle, every one of them is fent to a diftrict where he is an entire ftranger, and where he has no kind of connexions whatever.

We fet off at feven o'clock in the morning. The fouth gate by which we left the city is covered externally by a double baftion of a femi-circular form. We had confequently three gates to pafs before we were entirely without the walls. It is the only gate fortified in this manner that we have hitherto feen; for even thofe of *Pe-king* are only defended by a fingle baftion.

At

At a quarter paſt ten we came to *Li-ca-chong*, where we dined, and left it an hour and a quarter afterwards. At a quarter paſt four we arrived at the village of *Sau-yi-pu*, where we put up at a forry inn, after a day's journey of a hundred *li*. Our road lay chiefly over a plain, in ſome parts ſandy and full of ſtones. It took in general a ſouth direction, and carried us through a number of different places.

Near *Li-ca-chong* we croſſed a river, probably the fame we paſſed yeſterday near *Sin-cong-chen*. Its rapid ſtream, running to the ſouth-eaſt, is about two hundred and fifty yards wide. In the rainy ſeaſon it muſt contain a prodigious body of water, and accordingly an embankment of con- ſiderable height has been thrown up on each ſide, in order to prevent its inundating the neigh- bouring country. There is a diſtance of at leaſt three thouſand toiſes between the two embank- ments.

I remarked, in one of them, a handſome ſtone ſluice, which, when the river riſes to a certain height, carries a fertilizing ſtream into the ad- jacent fields. The pavement and the ſides of this ſluice conſiſt of large hewn ſtones. Its di- rection is ſerpentine, and its width about ſix feet.

It is shut by pieces of wood, one above another, let into a groove cut in the stones on both sides of the sluice. This sinuous shape proves that the architect perfectly understood how to weaken the rapidity of a stream, and was no stranger to the force of a body of water when propelled in a straight line.

In the afternoon we saw at a great distance to the westward, an insulated mountain with a castle on its summit, while to the eastward, at a great distance also, was a chain of mountains of little extent.

All the country we have this day travelled through consists of arable land, a great part of which having been sown in the autumn, begins already to be covered with a delightful verdure. In other places the husbandmen were ploughing, which gave us an opportunity of seeing the Chinese plough. Though very simple it is sufficient to turn up the strongest ground. I am resolved to buy one the first opportunity to carry out of the country with me, it being an excellent instrument for indifferent land. As to the harrow of the Chinese it seems to me to be inferior to ours because it has fewer teeth.

4th.

4th. We quitted our inn at three quarters paſt ſix, and an hour after paſſed at a little diſtance from the city of *Yeu-chin-gen* which is a ſmall place, and of which the exterior makes a very mean appearance.

At a quarter paſt eleven we came to *Kiang-v'ho-fau-y*, a village where we ſtopped and refreſhed. At twelve o'clock we quitted this laſt place of the province of *Chan-tong*, and at two *li* beyond paſſed its limits, and entered the province of *Kiang-nam*.

At a quarter paſt five we reached the village of *Tcheou-mou*, where we enjoyed a comfortable night's reſt, after a journey of a hundred and twenty *li* along a road which for the moſt part took a ſouth by eaſt direction.

The river which I mentioned the two preceding days, and which we again paſſed yeſterday evening at the entrance of the village of *Sau-y-pu*, over a ſtone bridge of five arches and Gothic conſtruction, was running on the eaſtern ſide of us during the whole of this day. Our road was very ſandy, very rugged, and very hilly in the province of *Kiang-nam*.

In the morning we met with orchards more extenfive, and confifting of taller trees, than any we had hitherto feen in China.

At a league to the weftward of *Tcheou-mou*, and upon the tabular fummit of a hill, ftands a large and noble convent, very agreeably fituated at fome diftance from the road. The edifice and its walls within which are three little groves of cedar and cyprefs, are in good repair. In the afternoon we faw a great many wild geefe and ducks:

5th. We proceeded on our journey at half after fix, and about five hours after arrived at the village of *Sang-hau-ché*, where we were to dine. The road was very rugged till we came within a league of the village, when we croffed a river by a bridge of hewn ftone, fix hundred paces long and twenty feet broad, having at leaft feventy openings, intended for the paffage of fmall veffels and covered over with flat ftones, which reft fimply upon pillars without arches.

North of the bridge ftands a large imperial pavilion. It is fquare and has a double roof, but it is in fuch bad condition that its walls are in ruin, and its roof fallen in. In the midft of it is

a ftone

a ſtone bearing an inſcription relative to the architect of the bridge, but the ſtone itſelf is in ſuch a ruinous ſtate that cords have been tied round it to prevent it from falling down.

Having croſſed the bridge we came to a dike or embankment, fully as handſome as thoſe in Holland, and at leaſt fifty feet thick at the top. The ſide towards the water deſcends with a great inclination, like the dikes made in the United Provinces within the laſt forty years; for it ſeems that it was not obſerved till then that the water has leſs action upon a ſurface much inclined, than upon a plane nearly perpendicular, and that by applying this principle to embankments they might almoſt always be preſerved from accident. The Chineſe, however, were aware of it from the firſt formation of their dams, and it appears alſo, that the keeping of them in good repair is here conſidered as a matter of the higheſt importance.

Half way between the bridge and the village of *Sang-hau-ché* ſtands, in the plain to the eaſtward, a large and magnificent convent, with edifices reſembling temples, the whole ſurrounded with a wall, which denotes that a great deal of care is taken of it.

When we had nearly reached our place of abode, we found upon the edge of the embankment a very lofty pillar, with a cage on the top, containing the head of a criminal executed on the 14th of February, by order of the Emperor, for having committed a robbery and murder in the village. His crime was infcribed upon a board nailed to the pillar.

Nearly oppofite *Sang-hau-ché*, which is fituated in the plain by the fide of the embankment, is the city of *Su-tfien-chen*, built upon the declivity of a high hill that ftands on the bank of the *Hoang-hau*, or the Yellow River.

In confequence of fome delay in the payment of our *Coulis*, it was two o'clock before we were able to proceed on our journey. Our road lay through cultivated plains, thickly interfperfed with great and fmall villages and hamlets. We alfo faw near the road to the eaftward a very handfome pagoda, confifting of ten diftinct buildings, all in excellent repair. At half paft five we came to the village of *In-hau-che*, where we are to pafs the night in a very comfortable houfe.

This place, which is pretty large, ftands near the Yellow River, by the fide of which we travelled

velled all the afternoon in a fouth-eaft direction, as I was enabled to perceive by the number of veffels that were failing up and down. We went this day a hundred and ten *li*.

Within thefe few days paft I have met with larger barrows than I ever faw before, and which, by the load they carried, might rather have been taken for carts. I obferved that the load occupied a fpace feven feet long by five feet wide. The wheel is at leaft four feet in diameter, and the barrow is drawn by an afs. Two barrow-men accompany it, one before to guide the animal, the other behind to keep the barrow in equilibrium. Some of them are tilted over (but with mats) like our carts, in order to fhelter the paffengers.

This evening our fecond conductor came to fettle the plan of to-morrow's journey. We determined to go ninety *li*, and confequently fhall have only thirty to travel the following day to *Von-ca-fen*, which will give us time to get on board our veffels the fame day.

6th. We fet off this morning at feven o'clock, in the midft of a thick fog, which was not difpelled till noon. Half an hour before it cleared away

away we reached *Tfong-hing-fyé*, where we dined. We left it at one o'clock in order to get to the village, where, according to our plan, we were to pafs the night, but the accommodations it afforded being very bad, the Ambaffador fuffered himfelf to be perfuaded by the fervants of the Mandarins to go as far as *Von-ca-fen*. We therefore proceeded on our journey at five o'clock. The wind blowing very ftrong, and the weather being exceedingly thick, our journey was very difagreeable. We were, however, fully indemnified, when, at a quarter paft eight we found ourfelves in very good and fpacious lodgings, although in a fmall town.

Our day's journey was a hundred and twenty *li*, our road running almoft always to the eaftward, and in the direction of the Yellow River. Upon the embankment by the fide of it we went, at two different times, a confiderable diftance. The top of it is ftill wider than that of the dike on which we were travelling yefterday, and is every where kept in the moft perfect order.

The Yellow River is the greateft of all thofe of the Empire of China, and its inundations are the moft formidable on account of the impetuofity of the ftream. Double embankments have therefore been thrown up on each fide in order to to prevent its ravages. The inner one is calculated for the ordinary rife of the water, and the outer one is meant to ferve on extraordinary occafions. The fuperintendance of thefe dams is entrufted to the care of three *Tfong-tous,* between whom the whole extent is divided; each of them being bound to refide in a city adjacent to the portion fubmitted to his infpeftion. In confequence of their holding this office they take the title of *Hau-cong Tfong-tou,* which anfwers to that of Intendant of Dikes in Holland.

7th. The weather was feverely cold. The wind, which had increafed a good deal during the night, was followed by heavy rain, and in the morning we had a great deal of thunder and lightning. At noon the wind fhifted to the north-weft and the cold augmented. A hard fhower of hail was fuperadded to the other meteorological phenomena, and was followed by large flakes of fnow which fell for a full hour.

In the afternoon the weather cleared up, but it continued to freeze during the whole of the night. We were therefore obliged to ftop all day at *Von-ca-fen,* for it would have been impoffible to crofs the river. Fortunately after having paffed it, we fhall have only four *li* to travel, in order to reach our veffels.

8th.

8th. The weather was fine and clear, but accompanied by a hard froft. The river, however, not being frozen, our baggage was conveyed acrofs it in boats, and put on board the veffels. At eight o'clock in the morning Fahrenheit's thermometer ftood at twenty-nine degrees, the wind being very fharp and piercing. At nine o'clock we paffed the river and arrived at ten at the town of *Sin-can-pu*, where we found our veffels waiting for us, and immediately embarked.

They were very large yachts, divided into feveral fpacious apartments, wherein we found ourfelves both comfortably and agreeably fituated: The Ambaffador and I had each our yacht, and two others were affigned to the five gentlemen in the fuite of the Embaffy.

Our baggage being tardily conveyed on board, it was four o'clock before we were able to get away.

Sin-can pu is a tolerably large place, fituated on the banks of a river, and full of handfome fhops, which befpeak a commercial place. It is alfo very populous.

When every thing was embarked we fet off with a fair wind, which affifted the effect of the ftream in carrying us down the river.

At

At fix o'clock we paffed the city of *Tfing-ho-chen*, a very extenfive place, where there is an Imperial cuftom-houfe, and where a *Hou-pou* is refident. A bridge of boats is laid acrofs the river, having a cable at one end, by means of which it is fuffered to fwing round with the ftream when a paffage is wanted for veffels, and is afterwards brought back from the bank, to which the current has drifted it, to the oppofite fhore, where it is again made faft by the cable. At the bridge the river is narrower than the Amftel, but is more frequented both by great and fmall veffels. It has on each fide a folid dike, and from one end of the city to the other its banks are entirely faced with hewn ftone.

At half paft feven we were already oppofite the town of *Houay-ngan-fou*, where we ftopped in order that our failors might be paid, and provifions be put on board for to-morrow. All the cities that lie in our route are bound to contribute their quota of thefe provifions.

It was eleven o'clock before we were able to fet off. The city of *Houay-ngan-fou* appears very large and populous; there is more than one breach in its walls which are in a very ruinous ftate, and the public buildings that we had an
opportunity

opportunity of feeing, feem not to be in much better condition.

On the weftern bank of the river, where there was a prodigious number of veffels, and fronting the city, is a large Imperial building with a ftone monument ftanding under it. This edifice, which is now mouldering into ruins, muft formerly have been very magnificent. It appears that the Chinefe fet little value upon their antiquities. The old things that do honour to their talents are in a manner abandoned to the deftructive hand of time without their fhewing any anxiety at their decay. Along the road we met with hundreds of thofe ftones, intended to preferve the remembrance of particular events in a ftate which proves the total neglect to which they are condemned, and the injuries they have fuffered from the inclemency of the air.

In the northern part of the city, and within the ramparts, ftands a kind of octagonal tower, the five ftories of which do not amount to an elevation of fixty feet, although the dimenfions of its bafe are in proportion to double that height.

While we were ftopping at *Houay-ngan-fou*, a great number of Imperial veffels paffed by loaded with

with rice for *Pe-king*. Thefe veffels, which are of confiderable fize, have two mafts; one placed very far forward, and the other two-thirds of their length from the ftern. Their lofty prow ftands up almoft vertically, and their bottom is flat, which gives them a fquare form, and renders them fit to carry confiderable burdens.

The canal was to-day of the fame width as yefterday, ftill running between two dikes or caufeways, which in fome places were entirely bordered with rufhes, in order to give more ftrength to the dam, and to oppofe the action of the water, which has a tendency to undermine the ground; an invention much refembling that of *Varech* in Holland.

This evening at nine o'clock we arrived off the city of *Pauin-chen*, where we ftopped in order that our people might enjoy a night's reft, of which they are much in need, our veffels being now pulled on by the tracking-line. At fun-rife we fet off again.

10th. I could diftinguifh very little of the city of *Pauin-chen*, which is, as I was told, very large, but deftitute of commerce. To-day, as well as yefterday, the direction of the canal was

to

to the south, while villages were scattered here and there along its banks.

In the morning we got sight of a considerable lake, at no great distance to the westward. It is so large in some places that we could hardly perceive its western shore. It was covered with a great number of large two-masted fishing boats, lying two and two together in order to haul the net at the same time, as is practised at Macao and along the coast. The lake is separated from the canal upon which we are navigating by a single dike that is not fifty feet broad, although the water of the canal is at least eight feet above the level of the lake. Along the edge of the latter the embankment is faced with a wall, made in part of hewn stone and partly of brick. Some repairs were going on there at the time we passed by. On the canal side the dike is also strengthened, in the way I have already mentioned, by reeds stuck into it in rows, the intervals between which are filled with strata of argillaceous earth, laid one over the other almost to the very top of the embankment; the whole being afterwards covered with a coat of clay a foot thick.

The surface of the country on the east side of the canal is at least ten feet lower than that of the

the water. It is excellent arable land, and for the moft part fit for the cultivation of rice. A great number of villages and hamlets prefent themfelves every moment to the eye, and afford a very pleafing profpect. In the eaftern embankment, flood-gates have been placed wherever neceffary. They are of hewn ftone, and exactly fimilar to thofe which I mentioned on the third of this month. We faw feveral of this kind, both yefterday and to-day. At half paft eleven we came abreaft of the village of *Fan-tfany-fan*, where we were obliged to ftop, becaufe the Mandarins had not furnifhed fufficient provifions for the fervants and the crews, or rather becaufe, according to cuftom, the domeftics of the Mandarins had fpeculated upon our allowance, and appropriated a part of it to their own ufe. The beft way of correcting them is the one we took, by ftopping, and giving them to underftand that we were determined not to be their dupes. A fupplement of provifions was immediately furnifhed us, and we again got under way.

We navigated the whole of the day along the fide of the lake, the ftream being in our favour, but as the wind was contrary, and it blew frefh, our progrefs was very flow. The cold obliged

obliged us to make ufe of braziers to warm our apartments.

The manner of fteering thefe veffels is very fingular, but well fuited to the nature of the paffage they have to make. Six or eight men track them on, while four others walk along the dike, carrying two light wooden anchors, the cables of which are faftened to ftrong ftancheons placed upon the decks. At the word given by the pilot, thefe anchors are dropped upon the ground, in order that the ftem or ftern of the veffel may be drawn towards the dike, according to the direction that it is wifhed fhe fhould take in her courfe, and thus to prevent her from being brought by the wind or the current with her broadfide to the ftream.

Their ropes of *rattan*, or, more properly fpeaking, of bamboo, are very ferviceable, becaufe they unite lightnefs and ftrength. Other cordage would be wanting in the firft, and even in the fecond quality, when neceffary to keep the veffel in the ftrength of the ftream. The ftancheons to which thefe ropes are made faft are the heavieft pieces of wood in the veffel, whofe whole depth they penetrate. There is one on each fide, both forward and aft.

The

The maſt is compoſed of two pieces, which are united at their head, but which, being ſeparated below from each other, are fixed in iron collars upon the two ſides of the veſſel, ſo that it may be brought down lengthwiſe upon the deck. There is at the ſame time at the foot of the maſt another piece of wood, alſo compoſed of two bits likewiſe joined at their upper end, where they form a crutch, upon which is placed a tackle for ſwaying up or lowering down the maſt; an operation by theſe means rendered extremely eaſy.

The rope by which the veſſel is tracked is made of the bark of bamboo: it is not thicker than the little finger, and yet it is very ſtrong, as well as very light. Of every production that grows in the vaſt extent of the Empire of China, there is undoubtedly none whoſe utility ſurpaſſes that of bamboo, which is employed on every occaſion, even as an article of food. Scarcely any thing is to be found in China, either upon land or water, in the compoſition of which bamboo does not enter, or to the utility of which it does not conduce. From the moſt valuable articles which ſerve to adorn the apartments of the Prince, down to the ſmalleſt tool handled by the meaneſt mechanic, bamboo is ſure to find a place. Houſes are entirely conſtructed of it, as well as all the furniture

furniture they contain. In navigation, it is bamboo which furnifhes every thing from the line that ferves to track the fmalleft fkiff, to the cable, that conftitutes the fecurity of the largeft veffel.

This tree, which is propagated with aftonifhing abundance, and grows with remarkable rapidity when planted in a favourable foil, deferves to be confidered as one of the greateft benefits that nature has conferred on the territory of China: the Chinefe accordingly fhew their gratitude by bringing it more and more into ufe. I doubt whether the vegetable kingdom in any part of the world affords a fubftance of fuch general utility as the bamboo, the qualities of which place it far above my panygeric.

We ftopped a part of the night, in order to give reft to our failors.

Setting off at day-break, we paffed, in the courfe of the morning, one of the extremities of the lake. A high wind which rofe in the afternoon compelled us to ftop.

The country, like that which we had feen during the preceding day, is entirely covered with hamlets and villages, and is in a high ftate of cultivation.

tivation. The wind having fallen, we got under-way again at midnight.

This morning at two o'clock we paffed the city of *Kau-yon-tcheou*, which we were prevented from feeing by the darknefs of the night. At fun-rife we came to *Van-tfu*, a tolerably large place; and at half paft feven reached the fuburbs of *Yang-tcheou-fou*, and ftopped mid-way before we came to the city, in the interval between the fuburbs and the convent of *Pe-ning-fau-tfi*.

I took this opportunity of going to fee the convent. The Chief Prieft and fix of the bonzes came out to pay me their refpects, and conducted me through the middle door to the firft temple. At my entrance about twenty bonzes ranged in two lines chanted a hymn. As I found myfelf near the altar, on which was the Emperor's chap, I performed before it the ceremony of adoration. I went afterwards to fee the fecond and third buildings of the temple, and was afterwards fhewn a ftone, with an infcription written in the prefent Emperor's own hand, and placed under a canopy in a feparate compartment. I vifited all the reft of the convent, which ferves as a habitation for at leaft fixty bonzes.

When I had feen every thing, the Chief Prieſt conducted me to the refectory, where he defired me to fit down at table and partake of fome fruit and tea. I accepted his invitation, and ſtaid there a quarter of an hour. The name of this prieſt is *Bonay-key*: he is fifty-five years old, but his appearance indicates a more advanced time of life. I thanked him on taking leave for the gracious reception he had given me, and made him a prefent for the convent. He attended me to the outfide of the gate.

The Gods of thefe pagodas are, 1. *Quang-ty*; 2. *Oyhait-ho*; 3. *Coun-yam*; 4. *Tfont-nay*; and, 5. *Mant-fu*. On both fides of the firſt ſtory are the four ufual figures of the guardians of temples, known by the name of *Ci-tay-tyem-cong*. On the fecond are alfo feen, on the two fides, eighteen images of ancient gods, called *Sapatlohong*. Thefe eighteen idols, and the five firſt mentioned, are all richly gilt, and half as large again as life.

Without the walls of the convent, by the fide of the river, is a magnificent triumphal arch of wood, with three paſſages, and with pedeſtals of white marble, fome of which were over-turned by the inundation of laſt year. It appears

as

as if they meant to leave them in their prefent ftate.

Almoft oppofite, on the weft fide of the river, ftands an Imperial monument under an hexagonal dome, which muft formerly have been a handfome edifice, but which is now beginning to moulder away.

Half an hour before we reached the fuburbs of *Yang-tcheou-fou,* we alfo faw two other Imperial Edifices, containing monuments. One is a pavilion with a triple roof, and the other an open hexagonal dome, fupported by columns. Both of them are beginning to decay, which is a truly afflicting fight, confidering the noble appearance they ftill make.

At one o'clock we fet off again, and for forty-five minutes continued to pafs along the walls of *Yang-tcheou-fou.* It appeared a very large place. Hundreds of fhips, yachts, and boats lined the fhore, and the crowd of people affembled on the two banks was innumerable.

At fome diftance below the city we paffed an octagonal tower of feven ftories, which were

not

not feparated from one another by any balcony or projection.

The *Hou-pou* of Canton, by whom his Excellency was complimented on board the Siam, having at prefent the chief fuperintendance of the Imperial magazines of falt of *Yang-tcheou-fou*, the Ambaffador and I difpatched our Interpreter to pay our compliments to him. He was fo pleafed with this, that in his turn he fent us one of the firft Mandarins of his fuite, commiffioned to prefent his beft wifhes for our happinefs, to offer us a confiderable prefent of fheep and other provifions, and to exprefs his regret at his not being able to wait on us in perfon, and wifh us a good journey to Canton.

We there learnt that the *Naa-fan-tayen*, our conducting Mandarin at *Pe-king*, has obtained an eminent poft, and that he has fet off for his refidence. He is called *Tfick-tfau-fou*; that is to fay, *Chief Director of the Manufacture of Raw Silk in the Provinces of Tché-kiang and Kiang-nam*, refiding at *Hang-tcheou-fou*. He confequently will not come as *Hou-pou* to Canton, his prefent place being fuperior to that employ.

In our way down the canal we faw feveral more pagodas, convents, and other public buildings belonging to the city of *Yang-tcheou-fou*.

At half paft four we perceived to the weft of us a magnificent temple dedicated to *Quang-ty*, with a convent by the fide of it. Thefe edifices are covered with green tiles, and kept in excellent repair.

A little beyond, at a place where the river divides into two branches, we came to a noble Imperial palace, furrounded by feveral lodges for the princes, and an octagonal tower, having on its top a great bar or rod of bronze, furrounded by circles or hoops, and terminating in a large ball of copper, the whole richly gilt. From the upper part of the rod, chains are brought down to the eight points of the roof, correfponding with the eight angles of the tower, to which eight little bells are attached. Thefe ornaments produce a moft beautiful effect. The tower is of the fame fize at top as at bottom, its walls being exactly vertical.

By the fide of this tower, is a temple ftanding under the fhade of old and tufted trees. Other trees planted round the whole of the building, add to the beauty of the fcene.—The tower being fituated situated opposite the canal, is seen from a very great distance

The principal entrance to this place is through three magnificent triumphal arches of stone, one of which stands in the front, and the other two on the sides of a great fore-court.

Every thing in this place announces the care taken of it by the bonzes, to whose trust it has been committed by the Emperor. The name of this summer palace, which is about fifteen hundred toises in circuit, is *Cau-ming-tsi*. It is pleasantly situated between two canals, and fronting a third, and is said to be eleven hundred and sixty years old, having been built in the reign of the Emperor *Yong-cong*.

At about five hundred yards from the principal entrance, and close to the water side, is a noble flight of stairs leading to the river; and opposite these stairs is an hexagonal dome supported by six pillars, in the midst of which is a stone bearing a long inscription.

Opposite to the building, and east of the canal, stands a convent, occupied by a number of bonzes.

This

This evening at feven o'clock we ftopped at thirty *li* beyond the place I have juft defcribed, oppofite another fummer palace called *Ong-uun*, which our conductors offered to fhew us. We mean to-morrow to avail ourfelves of their kindnefs; for this evening it is too late.

Among the crowds of curious fpectators who ftared at us to-day with eager eyes, the females were not the leaft numerous. We remarked a great difference between their demeanour and that of the women of *Chang-tong*. The female fex is here infinitely fairer, and of a more ruddy complexion. In the courfe of the day we remarked many pretty women, and particularly admired the family of a great Mandarin, which paffed by us in three large yachts. The charming women they contained ftood at the windows in fuch a way as to fee and be feen equally well. Three or four of them were perfect beauties. We may then fafely fay that we are ftill more unfortunate than Tantalus, fince to his torments our inflamed imagination added, in a delufive dream, the punifhment of the audacious Ixion.

13th. We went on fhore at an early hour in the morning to vifit the country houfe which I mentioned

tioned yesterday. The Emperor not having inhabited it for these twelve years past, it is much neglected; but if his Majesty were to testify the smallest desire to return to it, a fortnight would suffice to put every thing in order.

Even in its present state, this place is rendered worthy of attention by the variety of its edifices, by the diversity of the ground intersperfed with rocks, by its pavilions, its lakes, its bridges, &c. Every thing is disposed according to a system in which art seems to hide herself in the midst of the irregularities of nature; while the studied confusion of trees, fruit, flowers, and brambles compose a scene that seems due to chance alone. Already the birds enlivened the groves by their songs, and enriched the verdure with their plumage. Voluptuous summer, when thou hast spread thy charms over the country, what supreme delight must be tasted in this enchanting place.

No, it is not possible to give a faithful description of a Chinese villa. Every thing is intermingled, and seems on the point of being confounded; but the triumph of genius is to prevent the smallest disorder that might hurt the eye. Every instant a new combination affords a new variety, ſo much the more agreeable and ſtriking, as it has been the leſs poſſible to foreſee it; the ſpectator's ſurpriſe being conſtantly kept up, becauſe every moment produces a new ſcene. Perhaps plans and drawings might give an exact idea of their compoſition; but what plan can ſhew the order of that which is only perfect becauſe deſtitute of all order? What drawing can produce the effect of things which ſeem ſo diſcordant; and how is it poſſible to introduce into it that life which the different objects borrow from one another?— Our charming walk laſted an hour and a half.

From the dike we had an opportunity of ſeeing the adjacent country. The high lands, which are almoſt on a level with the embankment, are covered with a light tinge of green, already produced by the corn with which the fields have been ſown, while the low lands are preparing for the late harveſt of rice. The ſoil appears rich and fertile.

The great number of villages, hamlets, and habitations, have the double effect of enriching the landſcape, and of bringing to the mind the idea of proſperity and abundance. It was alſo eaſy to perceive from the crowd of people who flocked to ſee us, that the inhabitants

are

are strangers to poverty. We were now, indeed, travelling through the richeft parts of the Empire, while in our way to *Pe-king* we only croffed the leaft important diftricts of *Chang-tong* and *Tche-li*. *Kiang-nam*, *Tche-kiang*, and *Fo-king*, are the three principal provinces of China, becaufe they produce raw filk, the ftuff called nankin, and the different kinds of tea. When we fhall have feen the two former, we may flatter ourfelves with having had a fight of every thing that is the moft worthy of attention in China.

As I have mentioned thefe provinces, I cannot refrain from communicating to my reader the following obfervations, which they fuggeft.

White raw filk is principally a production of the north of *Tché-kiang*, though erroneoufly defignated by the name of *Nam-king*. The fouth parts only of *Kiang-nam* produce a fmall quantity.

The ftuff called *Nam-king*, which is manufactured at a great diftance from the place of that name, in the diftrict of *Fong-kiang-fou*, fituated in the fouth-eaft of the province of *Kiang-nam*, and upon the fea-fhore, is made of a brown kind of cotton, which it feems can only be grown in that quarter. The colour of *Nam-king* is then natural,

natural, and not fubject to fade. As the greater part of the inhabitants of Europe and other countries are in the perfuafion that the colour of the ftuff in queftion is given it by a dye, I am happy to have it in my power to rectify their error.

The opinion that I combat was the caufe of an order being fent from Europe a few years ago to dye the pieces of *Nam-king* of a deeper colour, becaufe of late they were grown paler. The true reafon of that change is not known: it was as follows:

Shortly after the Americans began to trade with China, the demand encreafed to nearly double the quantity it was poffible to furnifh. To fupply this deficiency, the manufacturers mixed common white cotton with the brown; this gave it a pale caft, which was immediately remarked, and for this lighter kind no purchafer could be found, till the other was exhaufted.

As the confumption is grown lefs during the laft three years, the mixture of cotton is no longer neceffary; and *Nam-king* is become what it was before. By keeping them two or three

years,

years, it even appears that they have the property of growing darker. This kind of stuff must be acknowledged to be the strongest yet known. Many persons have found that clothes made of it will last three or four years, although for ever in the wash. This it is that makes them the favourite wear for breeches and waistcoats both in Europe and America. The white *Nam-king* is of the same quality, and is made of white cotton as good as the brown, and which also grows in *Kiang-nam*.

Besides the above-mentioned stuffs, a great number of others are made in China, either of cotton, or different kinds of flax : among others, an immense quantity of callico, made of the cotton of Surat and Bengal, of which the English bring hither annually from forty to seventy thousand bales, which are almost entirely employed by the province of *Quang-tong*. Hence we may conceive what an enormous quantity of different kinds of stuff is manufactured and consumed in this Empire.

We have been obliged to stop to-day, because that part of the canal to which we are going on the other side of the *Kiang*, is blocked up by an
immense

immense number of Imperial boats laden with rice. We muſt then wait till a great part of them arrive here, and leave us room to paſs.

In the afternoon we have ſeen more than fifty paſs, for the moſt part ſo large, that they were capable of carrying more than three hundred thouſand weight of rice, although, to my great aſtoniſhment, they do not contain even a third of that quantity. From *Tſong-tchou*, fifty *li* from *Peking*, the rice is carried over land to the capital.

The canal on which we now are, and in which we have been navigating ever ſince we left the city of *Houay-ngan-fou*, is cut through a ſpace of more than a thouſand *li*, in order to abridge the route of theſe veſſels, although they only make one voyage *per* year. I have been aſſured that the Emperor has nine thouſand nine hundred and ninety-nine veſſels of this kind, from forty-five to a hundred feet long, and from twenty-two to twenty-five feet wide. Their crews, upon an average, conſiſt of twenty men each. The captains and pilots live on board with their wives and families, as is the caſe on board the veſſels of Cologne, in our own country. I remarked ſeveral very pretty women among them, and
others

others who carried their attention to their perfons fo far as to wear paint.

In thefe veffels, which are flat and fquare, the load is put at the bottom, and the upper part is laid out in cabins for the crew. A deck runs from one end to the other, and in the fides are ports or windows to give light to the apartments. The captain has the ftern of the veffel for his accomodation, and over him the pilot has his cabin. All the fore part is allotted to the failors. It is natural to fuppofe that all thefe people lead a very eafy life, being in the fervice and in the pay of the Emperor, and always at home, without any dread of encountering hard fatigue.

It is impoffible to refrain from obferving that economy is here of no account in the conveyance of rice. In other countries thefe veffels would be more heavily laden; or elfe, if that increafe of burthen would prevent their paffing every where, on account of the fhallownefs of the water, fmaller veffels would be built, which might be navigated by fewer men; and two voyages might be made annually inftead of one.

It is evident that the Emperor requires two hundred thoufand men for the conveyance of rice;

rice; and thefe men, as well as their families, are kept at the expence of the ftate. The quantity of rice fent annually to *Pe-king*, is more than feven hundred and fifty millions of pounds (French); a quantity truly aftonifhing. It is with this rice that the greater part of thofe who ferve in the army are paid, as well as thofe who are attached to the court. The whole of the above enormous quantity does not exceed what is wanted for that purpofe.

The greater part of the inhabitants of *Chantong*, *Tcheli*, and the more weftern provinces, do not make ufe of rice for their nourifhment, which is compofed of millet, and other productions of the earth, fuch as peas, &c.

All the provinces in which rice is cultivated are bound to deliver their contingent, or agricultural tithe, in the vicinity of *Kiang-nam*, where it is fhipped on board of the Imperial veffels. The province of *Quang-tong* is the only one exempt from this tribute, probably on account of the great number of troops it maintains, to whom rice is furnifhed for their fubfiftence.

It is in *Kiang-nam*, and principally in the diftrict of *Sou-tcheou-fou*, that all the veffels deftined for

for the conveyance of rice are built. Many of them are prettily painted, and ornamented with carve-work, and gilding. They have large fails hoifted upon their two mafts.

In the afternoon a veffel paffed us having ten Coreans on board in their way to *Pe-king*, whence they will be fent into their own country. They were fhipwrecked in a ftorm upon the coaft of China. I was liftening to a relation of that event, when the Coreans landed upon the dike. I went upon deck to fee them, and was much furprifed to find that as foon as they faw me, they ftretched out their hands, as if they knew me; ran to a fmall boat, and came alongfide of my yacht; but we were utterly unable to underftand one another. They then appeared to difcover their miftake, and were ftill more hurt when one of our Mandarins ordered them to retire, and to proceed on their journey. I prefume that fome of them had feen, or known fome of the Dutch at Japan, whither the Coreans make a voyage every year, and that they took me for one of their old acquaintance.

This evening a ftrong north wind has fprung up, and the weather is very cloudy.

14th. The

14th. The rice-veffels hindered us again to-day from continuing our journey.

15th. We fet off at the break of day; but with the intention of not going farther than to one *li* on this fide of the *Kiang*, which is here exceedingly wide. We are to pafs it; but its furface being much agitated by a frefh breeze from the north-weft, we are prevented from doing fo, and muft wait a more favourable moment. A heavy rain at the fame time prevents us from going afhore to take a walk.

Having this morning feen a pretty large veffel go by, laden with the bones of animals, I was defirous of knowing for what purpofe they were intended; and was told that they are to be burnt, and that the cinders are to be put upon the ground fown with rice, when the plant is about a foot high, and before the water is let into the fields. It is affirmed that this practice renders the land very fertile, which indeed cannot be doubted, fince bones contain a great deal of the faline and oily principles. It is well known, befides, that all kinds of afhes make excellent manure.

I have feen lime fpread in the fame manner, upon the land that grows rice between Canton and Macao; but it is when the plant is two feet high, and after the grounds have been inundated.

16th. A gentle rain has continued to fall all this day. The rice veffels ftill obftructing our paffage, we fhall ftay another day here. It is very lucky, while thus detained, that we are fo well lodged.

I obferved in the laft eighty or a hundred *li* that we have travelled, that we frequently met with great heaps of reeds piled up along the dike. This led me to afk if that flexible fhrub grew hereabout; and I was told that immenfe quantities fhoot up in the neighbourhood of lakes and moraffes at no great diftance to the weftward. Hence it feems that nature has taken care to place the reed in places where it is wanted to confolidate the dikes.

17th. At the break of day we fet off in order to quit the canal, and enter the *Kiang*, in point of extent the fecond river in the Empire, and at that place very wide. It ran down very flowly at the time we entered it, no doubt becaufe its ftream was checked by the flood-tide. The banks of the river were level, and thickly planted with trees; but at fome diftance to the fouth,

and

and fouth-weft we faw a great many mountains, which ftretched away to the eaftward, and approached the river in that direction.

Shortly after our departure, we paffed the city of *Qua-tcheou,* fituated to the northward. It is furrounded with very extenfive walls, which in feveral places, however, fhew marks of decay. The embankment ftands exactly between the city and the river.

Half a league beyond, we coafted along a very lofty ifland, compofed of rocks, and fituated near the fouthern bank. The weft fide of it comes floping down, but the oppofite one is almoft perpendicular. This ifland, called *Kiang-tfang-tfi,* was chofen by one of the Emperors for a country retirement; and feveral edifices were accordingly erected upon it, which when feen from the weftward, afford a very agreeable profpect, and have all the appearance of a fmall town. All the buildings on that fide ftand on the declivity of the rock, and in a manner upon one another. They are conftructed of brick; and the roofs are of green and yellow varnifhed tiles. Some of them are, however, covered with the common red kind.

L 3

We

We perceived, on the fummit of the rock feveral domes, and to the north, a handfome tower in good repair, and fimilar to that of *Cauming-tfi*. There are buildings wherever its declivity permits any to ftand; and as it is perpendicular on the eaft fide, the handfome buildings that front that way, which are the principal Imperial edifices, are conftructed upon a level fpot at the foot of the rock. The landing-place being to the north, a flight of broad ftone fteps has been placed there, coming down clofe to the water-fide. A baluftrade, alfo of ftone, intended to prevent accidents, extends along the fide of the road, which itfelf runs round the whole of the ifland, and paffes over vaulted channels, that ferve to carry off the rain. In other places, where breaches in the rock interrupted the road, the chafms have been filled up with mafonry, in order to render it level and commodious. Laftly, to give ftill more fecurity to paffengers, another baluftrade borders the top of the rock, to the eaftward, in the part where the fteep defcent begins. Several magnificent buildings ftand upon the fummit.

On the eaftern fide, the river has wafhed up earth, and formed the flat beach which I have mentioned above, and on which gardens have been

been made, planted with shrubs and flowers. Their pleasing appearance enlivens the magnificent prospect afforded by the edifices in front of which they are situated. The island appears very populous, and the outside of the buildings bespeaks the hand of care.

Upon the upper part of the rock are a great many forest trees, standing between the buildings and overlooking the roofs. The whole composition gives this place the appearance of one of those landscapes in which the painter has assembled all the objects most pleasing to the eye. I sketched two drawings of it, one representing the eastern part, the other the western, with the intention of having them finished by the painter I employ at Canton.

About three *li* farther eastward than this island begin the suburbs of *Ching-kiang-fou*, built among rocks by the water-side.

At a small distance from the road, upon the summit of a mountain, stand a temple and a convent, which must afford a pleasing view when seen from the island of *Kiang-tsang-si*.

While abreast of these suburbs, we entered into a canal, which is about two hundred toises long, and which is separated from the river by a lofty and handsome embankment bordered with reeds, and communicating with the ditch dug round the city. In this place the passage being only the width of two vessels, we were obliged to haul in our yacht by means of the capstan, between the side of the canal and the rice vessels which lined the opposite bank. Having gone some distance along this canal, we passed through a sluice of hewn stone of dimensions scarcely exceeding the breadth of a rice vessel.

It would seem that in China they have no idea of flood-gates; for all those I have seen are closed by planks, in the way I have already mentioned. These planks are disposed like the beams in front of the sluices in Holland.

We waited in this canal or sluice for the rise of the tide, which detained us till half past two in the afternoon. We then proceeded on our journey, being tracked by a dozen men along the side of this narrow canal, which was constantly blocked up by the rice-carriers. After having travelled for some time in this manner, we arrived

at

at the north-weſt baſtion of the city, where ſeveral flags were flying upon the baſtion; while a great number of ſoldiers ſtood in the embraſures founding conchs in the place of trumpets. This was the firſt time that I had ever heard a Chineſe blow one of theſe ſhells. It is well known that they are uſed as a warlike inſtrument in the iſlands of the South Sea.

On the outſide of the baſtion is a very lofty bridge of hewn ſtone, of a ſingle ſemicircular arch. I was aſtoniſhed at the bad repair of this bridge, conſidering its conſtant utility, and the crowds of people that paſs over it.

We continued for a great while longer to follow the ramparts of the city, which muſt conſequently be a place of great extent. It is inhabited both by Tartars and Chineſe. When we came to the ſouth-weſt end of it, we again found flags, ſoldiers, and conchs upon the baſtion. Beyond it is a bridge ſimilar to that at the north-weſt end of the town, and quite as much neglected. Shortly after we paſſed through a ſluice of the ſame kind as that which we had met with in the morning.

At

At the end of the southern suburbs are two triumphal arches of stone, while upon a hill at a little distance stands an hexagonal tower in very good condition. It is seven stories high, has a long spire upon the top of it, and is plainly distinguishable from the canal.

A little way beyond the latter stands a large convent, with a temple, a great variety of other buildings, and a flight of stairs of hewn stone, leading from it down to the water-side. The whole appeared to be kept in excellent order.

On the outside of the city the ground grew uneven, and a little beyond it the mountains began to make their appearance.

In passing along the canal I observed a number of Chinese in small boats employed in deepening it, by means of an iron machine, about a foot long. It consists of two spoons or ladles, fitting close to each other, and opening and shutting by means of two long handles of bamboo, like a pair of tongs. With this machine they bring up the mud or clay from the bottom, and when the boat contains two barrow fulls, its load is thrown out upon the shore. Economy does not seem to be at all consulted in this operation.

The

The number of spectators of both sexes who crowded to see us go by was inconceivable. It was night before we had passed all the rice barges, and seven o'clock before we stopped to take our repast; after which we continued our journey during the whole of the night.

18th. At three o'clock in the morning we reached a village extending a great distance upon the top of the dike and alongside of the canal as far as a lofty bridge of stones, under which we passed. At half past seven we came to the city of *Tang-yang-chen*, where we were detained two hours, while changing trackers and taking provisions on board.

Setting off again at half past nine, we ranged round three sides of the city, keeping close to the ramparts, and passed under three lofty stone bridges which stand near three gates of the city, and of which the arches describe a semicircle.

The space inclosed within the walls is considerable; but it is to be presumed that the whole surface is not built upon. The suburbs made no appearance, nor was there any thing remarkable, unless the great number of inhabitants.

During

During the morning we paſſed by ſeveral ſluices of hewn ſtone cut through the dike, and all in ſuch a ruinous condition as to be unſerviceable. I was much ſurpriſed to ſee things of ſo great importance in ſuch diſorder, while the ſtones which had been detached by the action of the water, would ſuffice to repair them. This neglect is no doubt attributable to the Mandarins, who appropriate the money that ought to be employed in repairs to their own uſe.

At the end of the ſouth-weſt ſuburbs, and in a place named *Chéle* is a ſuperb convent, temple, and other edifices equally magnificent. A little beyond is a lofty ſtone bridge, after which we came to another convent called *Hauy-hau-tſi*, a ſtill larger and more beautiful building than the laſt; and near the temple, which is conſecrated to the God *Quangty*, is a noble octagonal tower of ſeven ſtories, and of the ſame conſtruction as that of *Cau-ming-tſi*. This tower ſtanding near the canal I was the better able to diſtinguiſh its point and ſpire.

I then perceived that it was made of ſome ſort of caſt metal. The Chineſe aſſured me that it is a particular kind of very pure and very valuable iron; but that the ball at the end is of copper.

The

The iron rod, as well as I could judge, is twenty feet long, and is confequently of no inconfiderable weight. It is fixed in a bafe or conical focket, alfo very long, which immediately above the roof contracts to a fize little more than equal to that of the rod itfelf, to which it ferves as a fupport, and to the length and weight of which it is adapted. Round the rod and one above another, are placed feven hoops or rings, the middle one of which is the largeft, while the others decreafe in diameter, in proportion as they are removed from it towards the extremities. All the feven are confined by crofs pieces of iron proceeding from the rod. Over all thefe hoops, and almoft at the end of the rod, is a plate in the form of a ftar, from each of the eight points of which hangs a little bell and a chain that defcends to each of the eight angles of the roof. Below thefe angles larger bells are fufpended, befides fome that hang to the middle of each chain. Finally, the rod is terminated by a large ball of metal gilt. This manner of ornamenting the top of towers renders them very confpicuous, and gives them a moft magnificent appearance.

This convent has a feparate building belonging to it, ftanding by its fide, and formerly inhabited by a Chriftian, a native of the eaft, named *Kiam-*
long-

long-citay-ouang, whofe family came originally from *Tai-kiam-cok*, and who was canonifed by the Chinefe after his death. His image is worfhipped here, as well as in feveral pagodas.

This convent and tower are fituated fronting the canal. They are feen from a great diftance, and even from the city of *Tang-yang-chen*, prefenting a very noble object to the eye. The canal defcribes a femicircle round thefe buildings; and when oppofite the fouth-fide of them refumes a ftraight direction, by means of which the traveller continues to enjoy a view of the tower for a long time.

At this part of the canal we met with a repetition of the obftructions occafioned by the rice fhips bound to *Pe-king*, which blocked up one half of the channel.

The road being now clear of the crowds that had followed our yacht from the city, I landed, in order to take a walk upon the embankment by the fide of the canal, and to get a view of the neighbouring country. The profpect is delightful on all fides, and the appearance of the country is that of a well-cultivated garden, being every where flat, and fown with corn, which begins

gins already to fhew itfelf above the furface. The level of the land is at leaft ten feet above the furface of the canal, and interfected by large canals and ditches full of water. The ground, which is of an argillacious nature, appears very fertile and of eafy cultivation. The corn here has a thick ftalk, and large and numerous leaves, which are a fufficient proof of the goodnefs of the foil.

I obferved that in fome fields, and in particular fpots, the corn was fown in little furrows croffing each other at right angles; in others the feed was fet in a right line by means of a drill *(femoir)*; and laftly, there were fome places, but a very few, which appeared to have been fown by the hand, as with us, and in general in narrow beds, with little paths between them, as in the kitchen-gardens of Holland. All thefe diverfified plantations cheer the eye, and the whole is as free from weeds as our pleafure-gardens.

As far as the eye could reach the whole country was crowded with farms and habitations; and figns of abundance and profperity were every where vifible. The houfes were all built of bricks and covered with tiles. There feemed however to be a fcarcity of cattle; for during

during my walk, which lasted an hour and a half, I only saw a single cow.

It is easily perceivable here that the canal is the work of art, not only because it runs in a straight line, but also because its banks have been raised by the earth taken out of it till they are at least twenty feet above the level of the water. The top of these embankments is barely of the width necessary for a path. Towards the fields the slope is sown with corn almost all the way up.]

The peasantry here are a good looking race, and are very well clad.

To the eastward the distant view is bounded by mountains situated towards the sea coast, all the rest is a plain as far as the north-west, where the hilly country that surrounds *Nam-king* contracts the horizon.

In no part of the world does the traveller meet with prospects similar to those which every part of this country affords.

In the afternoon we saw several brick-kilns placed along the top of the embankment.

At

At half paſt three we were abreaſt of *Li-fang*, a pretty large place, which, owing to the number of its ſhops, and the good condition of its houſes, made a very pleaſing appearance. There we paſſed firſt through a ſtone ſluice, with two openings, ſeparated in the middle by a very ſtrong mound of hewn ſtone, and afterwards under a ſtone bridge of great elevation, and the beſt of all thoſe we had met with for two days paſt.

Not far from *Li-fang* is a ſmall pagoda, kept in very good repair. We ſtopped at ſix o'clock to take our repaſt, and continued our voyage afterwards during the whole of the night.

19th. At three o'clock in the morning we came to the city of *Chang-tcheou-fou*, and it was ſix before we reached the extremity of the ſuburbs. This may ſerve to give ſome idea of the length of the town. The cold was ſo ſevere during the laſt night that the fields, trees, every thing in ſhort was covered with a white froſt.

South of the city the canal increaſed to double its former width. The earth produced by its excavation, and in general thrown upon its banks, has in this part been carried away, probably in

Vol II.   M   order

order to be employed for some particular purpose, or perhaps, as it is of an argillaceous nature, it may have been made into bricks for some public buildings.

The banks are here higher than the adjacent country, nor did we see so many farms as yesterday; but villages and hamlets of good appearance, with houses built of stone and covered with tiles are more frequent. At seven o'clock I counted thirty-one villages or other places within the circle taken in by my eye, and several of the number were of considerable magnitude.

The fields in this part of our route lay lower than those we saw yesterday. The water of the ditches and trenches has a free communication with the principal canal by means of several navigable canals which branch off on either side.

At eight o'clock we passed by *Tchi-tsi-yen*, which occupies both sides of the canal, and which has all the appearance of a little city. Two ditches dug to the eastward and westward communicate here with the canal, and over each of them is a lofty stone bridge in very good condition, while a third bridge stands across the canal itself; with a passage, but no arch. The

facing

facing of the piers is of hewn ſtones, placed perpendicularly one upon another, to the height of about twenty feet, with planks laid over them.

The direction of the canal made by human labour from the city of *Tchun-con-fou* is nearly in a right line from ſouth-eaſt to north-weſt, except near the city of *Tang-yang-chen*, where it makes a deflexion, becauſe no doubt that city exiſted before the digging of the canal, and a ſmall ſtream or natural river rendered an artificial channel an unneceſſary work.

It is evident that this canal was not cut till after the epoch when the imperial reſidence was removed from *Nam-king* (which ſignifies the *South Palace*) to *Pe-king* (the *North Palace*), and when it was certain that the Emperor had abandoned his former abode. It is, then, to be preſumed that the canal was dug four hundred years back, ſince *Pe-king* became the capital of the Chineſe Empire four hundred and twenty-five years ago.

As the country is flouriſhing, the temples are numerous, and kept in better order than in the arid regions of the weſt through which we paſſed before.

before. The number of bonzes fettled here proves that they are under no apprehenfions as to a fubfiftence.

At a quarter paft nine we paffed by the village of *Quon-li-tchan*, ftanding on the oppofite fides of the canal. It is a moderately large place, and very populous, as was proved incontrovertibly by the crowds of curious fpectators with which both banks were lined. *Tchi-ifi yen* and *Quon-li-tchan* contain triumphal arches of ftone, the rude workmanfhip of which befpeaks their antiquity. In the firft of thefe places there is one, and two in the village, including that which ftands within the walls of an old pagoda, no doubt in honour of the faint who is worfhipped there.

In the morning we paffed by a convent and a temple, dedicated to the goddefs *Coun-yam*, with buildings belonging to them, kept in very good repair. In a fmaller temple, ftanding by the fide of the former, is the ftatue of the Chriftian faint *Kiam-lang-citay-ouang*, whom I mentioned yefterday. As we were going by I got a fight of the ftatue, which is coloffal and entirely gilt.

Half an hour afterwards we came to *Loo-fa-tchen*, a very large place fkirting both fides of the canal.

canal. At no great distance from it is a great pagoda, dedicated to *Sam-coun-thong*, and two ancient triumphal arches of stone.

This morning we saw a chain of mountains at a great distance to the north-east. My telescope enabled me to distinguish two castles built on two of the highest parts of the ridge.

At three in the afternoon we had an insulated mountain, called *Y-tchun-chan*, standing to the westward of us at the distance of four or five *li*. Upon its summit are two pagodas, which, notwithstanding their immense height at which they stand, and the difficulty of approach, appeared to me, when I examined them with my telescope, to be kept in very good repair. The foot of the mountain, which forms a declivity of ten or twelve *li* long, is covered with hundreds of houses, standing detached from one another, and all coated with plaster, the whiteness of which, contrasting with the green of the mountain, gives them a very striking appearance. In a hollow in the mountain itself stands a habitation entirely overshadowed with trees, another marks the middle of the ascent, and between that and the summit a third seems to indicate three-fourths of the total elevation. All these situations appear agreeable.

South-

South-east of this mountain is another much lower, having on its summit a convent and a temple; and by the side of them an octagonal temple, constructed like that of *Cau-ming-tsi*, except that instead of the metal spire and its ornaments it has nothing on the top of it but a large ball. This convent is called *Houay-tchun*. At some distance beyond, and between these two mountains is a handsome country-house, known for a thousand years by the name of *Ngok-si-fau-uun-tsi*, which was that of its original owner, a Mandarin of very high rank, whose virtue and unshaken fidelity could not save him from decapitation. Accused before the Emperor *Long-can-tsong*, he was condemned to death. The calumny being shortly after discovered, the body of the unfortunate Minister of State was interred by order of the same Emperor with all imaginable pomp, and a magnificent monument was erected over his grave. The monarch gave him besides the title of *Saint*, and conferred honours upon his son, at the same time that his perfidious accusers were punished with death. This magnificent tomb is in the province of *Tche-kiang*, near the city of *Hang-tcheou-fou*, where we shall probably have an opportunity of seeing it.

At

At four o'clock we reached the fuburbs of *Von-fi-chen*, in the neighbourhood of which we faw at leaft a dozen pagodas. Five of them are clofe to the town, and are at the fame time very near to one another. One of them ftands upon a little ifland fituated in the middle of the canal, which here grows wider, and even appears to be a branch of a river. In the fuburbs is a convent of nuns or female bonzes, as alfo a large and very beautiful triumphal arch ftanding between two houfes in a court or little empty fpace.

It is impoffible to conceive the number of people that crouded to get a fight of us, fome on fhore and others in little boats, by which we were entirely furrounded.

The fuburbs are interfected by feveral ditches. The houfes of which they are compofed are fo many fhops, filled for the moft part with pottery of all kinds and qualities, fuch as urns, vafes, pots, tiles, &c. It appears that thefe articles are manufactured in the environs. There is alfo a brick-ground and a place intended for the repair of veffels. At half paft four we came to the gate of the city, and made a ftop there, that being the place where our failors were to be paid.

According

According to the information I was able to obtain, the city of *Vou-fi-chen* is a large place, well built, neat, and full of inhabitants. Of this laft circumftance we were well affured by the multitude that furrounded us.

At feven o'clock, every thing being arranged, our tracking line was ftretched anew; and towed us on without intermiffion during the reft of the night.

Before it grew dark I obferved to the fouth of the city a very noble and lofty tower, alfo re-fembling that of *Cau-ming-tfi*.

At eight o'clock the mafters of our veffels had orders to ftop till to-morrow morning. Our firft conductor is gone to *Sou tcheou-fou*, in order to arrange things for our reception with the governor of that city, where an Imperial entertainment is to be given us, and where it is intended to fhew us the curiofities of the place. It is probable that we fhall arrive there to-morrow.

29th. At break of day the tracking line again put the yacht in motion, and we continued our courfe along the canal, which ftill keeps a fouth-eaft direction. In general the country is

more

more uneven than yefterday, owing to a number of hills and mounts, indicating graves. The villages are lefs numerous, but there are more fmall cuts and ditches communicating with the great canal. Trees were in fuch abundance as often to conceal diftant objects from our fight.

At nine o'clock we came to the town of *Mong-ting*, a pretty large place. Two hours and a half afterwards we came to *Sou-tcheou-huye-quan*, a vaft and populous place, where there is a ferry, and a *Hou-pou's* hotel, ftanding in the middle of the town upon the bank of the canal, and producing a very good effect.

Having paffed this place we perceived, at a little diftance to the weftward, a chain of mountains, which feemed to run in the fame direction as the canal beyond the city of *Sou-tcheou-fou*.

In the morning feveral convents and temples, the two handfomeft of which ftand exactly at the extremity of *Sou-tcheou-huye-quan*, engaged our attention. I perceived fome edifices by the fide of a very lofty tower, on the top of a mountain called *Ling-on-chan*, at a great diftance to the fouth-eaft, and was affured that they made part of a fummer palace built there by one of the Emperors

perors while the Imperial refidence was ftill in this province.

" To the fouth-eaft alfo, and likewife at a diftance, ftand a tower and a convent upon a mountain called *Chang-on-chan.*

Eight *li* beyond *Sou-tcheou-huye-quan,* another narrow canal branches off from that on which we are travelling to the weftward; and is only feparated from it by a quay about fix feet wide, which had formerly a facing of hewn ftone on each fide, and which is now in very bad condition in feveral parts, without any attention appearing to be paid to it.

Nobody was able to tell me what was the motive for building this quay, the conftruction of which muft have coft a great deal of money, and which appears to me perfectly ufelefs, fince ftone bridges have been erected at convenient diftances to facilitate the communication between the two canals. As to myfelf I was utterly unable to conjecture with what view fuch a work could have been undertaken.

At half paft twelve we paffed by the graves of two perfons of diftinction. Near the tombs, and by by the fide of the path that leads to them, are placed five pair of ftatues fimilar to thofe which I have already mentioned; that is to fay, two lions fitting, two rams lying down, then two horfes, two elephants, and two Mandarins ftanding. Tombs are very numerous in this place, and for the moft part ftand under fmall clumps of cedar and cyprefs.

At one o'clock we left, at a certain diftance from us to the eaftward, *Sou-tcheou-hou-yau-chan*, built upon a hill. In the centre of it is a handfome octagonal tower, feven ftories high, an idea of which may be formed from that of *Cau-mingtfi*. Buildings placed one above another give to this fpot fo ftriking a refemblance to the weft fide of the little ifland of *Kiang-tchang-tfi*, which I mentioned on the 17th of this month, that a defcription of one may ferve for the other; for here alfo the charming environs prefent a moft delightful picture to the eye.

At two o'clock we landed at *Sou-tcheou-caupan-kiou*, a pretty large and very populous place. So many aqueducts and canals are here feen, that it may be faid to ftand in the midft of the water; that of the principal ditches wafhing the

foundations

foundations of the houses, which are all of hewn stone.

We there passed under three capital bridges built of stone. Yesterday and to-day we met with thirty others of similar construction, which we either left on one side of us, or through which we passed.

Sou-tcheou-eau-pau-kiou contains several temples and convents in good condition, as well as three triumphal arches of stone. It was past three o'clock before we reached the further end of the town. An immense multitude of both sexes was assembled all along our road, and the houses were filled from top to bottom with people crowding on one another to get a sight of us, which procured us in our turn the pleasure of seeing the pretty faces of several belles. Most of them were painted, which appears here to be so prevalent a custom, that it even obtains among children of three or four years old. The white in particular is so glaring, that it is no exaggeration to say that a face covered with it may be distinguished at the distance of a hundred yards. A complexion of this kind is so unlike that of nature, that it seems more calculated to disgust than to please.

The

The rouge ufed in China is in general better than that of Europe. A woman whofe fkin is tolerably fair and fmooth, and who is not in the habit of laying on white, might with this rouge imitate the frefh colour of youth, without its being poffible for the action of heat or cold to difcover the artifice, even to the moft penetrating eye; nor would the habitual ufe of it in this moderate way have any bad effect upon the fkin. It is in this manner that all cofmetics ought to be ufed, in order that thefe fecret arts, intended to make women appear more agreeable and fafcinating in the eyes of their admirers, may not be betrayed by a ridiculous affectation; and that this practice may not deftroy the advantages of a fmooth and foft fkin. We might then confent to forgive the fair an artifice which would be no longer pernicious, and which would find its excufe in the defire of increafing the paffion of a lover, or of moving the indifferent heart.

At four o'clock we paffed by the village of *Houang-ton-fang*, where there are two ftone bridges, one of them being of three arches and having a pavilion in the middle, intended, no doubt, to enable the traveller to reft himfelf, and the inhabitant of the town to enjoy the frefh air.

In

In this village a trade is carried on in brown earthen veffels, which are feen piled up in the form of very lofty pyramids in the front of the fhops.

We were obliged to turn off on one fide in order to go from *Sou-tcheou-cau-pau-kiou* to the village of *Houang-ton-fang*, becaufe the ufual canal from this firft place till within a fhort diftance of the city of *Sou-tcheou-fou*, is entirely obftructed by rice veffels.

At five o'clock we reached the entrance of the fuburbs of *Sou-tcheou-fou*, where we paffed under a bridge of three arches, of a conftruction equally noble and elegant. It would be impoffible to build a handfomer, even of marble. Each pier ftands upon a maffive fquare of a fingle ftone, fomewhat longer than the breadth of the bridge, which appeared to me to be eighteen feet in the clear, and on both fides of which is a handfome ftone baluftrade. The admirable workmanfhip of this bridge gives it a very agreeable appearance. The piers of the middle arch are not more than two feet and a half thick at the bottom; and in every refpect it would do honour to the moft able architect in Europe. A quarter of an hour afterwards we came to another ftone-
bridge,

bridge fimilar to the former, but of only a fingle arch. Oppofite was the place appointed for our veffels to ftop before a large quay, upon which, before our arrival, a ftrong guard of foldiers was already pofted. Their tents were pitched along the quay, in order to prevent the curiofity of the people from being troublefome to us. This precaution, indeed, was very neceffary, as without it our veffels would have been funk by the weight of thofe that would have crowded on board.

Soon after our arrival our firft conductor fent the *Lingua* to the Ambaffador and me, to inform us that to-morrow morning at ten o'clock the ceremonial would take place in the city, and that palanquins would be fent for our conveyance. We were confequently requefted to hold ourfelves in readinefs, as well as the gentlemen in the fuite of the Embaffy who are to accompany us.

21ft. At nine o'clock in the morning the Mandarins came to us to beg us to make our entry into the city. We repaired there accordingly in our palanquins, as well as the gentlemen in our fuite. We were carried by four *Coulis*, and they by only two.

We

We paffed through feveral ftreets well paved, but narrow, and full of fhops of little confequence. Curiofity had every where affembled prodigious crowds, and if care had not been taken to plant centinels at the top of the crofs ftreets, we moft affuredly fhould not have reached the place of our deftination. We were defired to alight at a houfe near the place they were pleafed to call the Imperial court. About a quarter of an hour afterwards a meffenger was fent to conduct us to that edifice, before which the troops were drawn up in a line. We were immediately conducted to the hall containing his Imperial Majefty's *chaft*, oppofite which we performed the ufual ceremony of proftration. We then paid our refpects to the *On-tcha-tfu* and governor of the town. (The *Fou-yuen*, who generally refides here, is abfent.) They told us that the Emperor had been very well fatisfied with our Embaffy, and found us perfons of fo much fincerity, that he had given orders to prepare an entertainment for us, to make us prefents, and to treat us with all poffible refpect; orders with which they were very happy to comply.

The Mandarins then begged us to feat ourfelves upon cufhions to fee a play acted, which was immediately ordered to begin. Scarcely had we

fet

fet down, when a little table was fet before each of us, covered with fruits and delicacies of all forts. Thefe were afterwards removed to make room for difhes of hot meat, dreffed in the Chinefe manner, which we did not touch, becaufe our cooks were preparing us a repaft.

The actors were dreffed as magnificently as any we had feen, and played *extempore*, merely to amufe us, and without any fettled plan. It was paft twelve when we rofe in order to take our dinner in another apartment. The *On-tcha-fu* had retired, but the Governor came and joined us. His Excellency begged him, through the medium of our Interpreter, to favour us with a fight of the public buildings, and whatever other curiofities the city might contain. He anfwered that there was little worth feeing, but that he would comply with our requeft as foon as we fhould have dined. It is a cuftom among the Chinefe, as well as the other nations of the Eaft, to depreciate every thing belonging to themfelves, and to fpeak of it as fomething very common, at the fame time that they lavifh undeferved praife upon all that is fhewn them by foreigners. We had heard fo much faid of *Sou-tcheou-fou*, which is a place of great celebrity, that we confidered the Governor's anfwer as mere words of courfe, and during

during the whole of our repaſt were taken up with nothing but the idea of the intereſting things we were about to ſee. Our dinner being over, we ſeated ourſelves again in our palanquins.

After having paſſed through ſeveral ſtreets of the city, we were carried a great way off to a ſmall convent and a pagoda, with a garden belonging to it, in which a mount has been thrown up, in imitation of a rock. The temple dedicated to the goddeſs *Coun-yam* was little deſerving of our attention, and all the reſt was not worth the trouble of looking at. Half an hour was more than ſufficient to examine this *beautiful* edifice. We were afterwards requeſted to take tea; but we thanked the bonzes for their obliging offer, telling them that it was our intention to viſit ſome other curioſities.

It was then propoſed to ſhew us another temple; but the Ambaſſador, hearing that it was inferior to the former, refuſed to go. The Mandarins, who were our conductors, appeared embarraſſed, as if they did not know whither to conduct us. I had ſome things written down in a liſt, which I ſubmitted to their inſpection; but they found an objection to every one of them:

ſome-

sometimes it was the distance, sometimes the disorder the place was at present in, and sometimes the badness of the road. Thus, every thing considered, we had nothing better to do than to return to our yachts, without having obtained any gratification of our curiosity; and this was what we resolved to do.

The height of the artificial mount of which I have spoken, having enabled me to overlook a great part of the city, I observed several spots of cultivated ground in the north-east quarter. The circumference of this city is estimated at thirty-six *li*; and it is said to be very populous. According to the report of the Chinese, it is very commercial; contains a great number of manufactories; and is the residence of many opulent merchants. We were not able to ascertain the truth of this information, any more than that of the very popular opinion, which represents this city as the principal seat of sensuality in China. It is asserted that the fair sex is here more beautiful than in any other part of the Chinese dominions; and that the women of *Sou-tcheou-fou* have in that respect obtained for their native city a reputation which no other can dispute.

Every one alſo ſpeaks of *Sou-tcheou-fou, Hong-tcheou-fou,* and *Quang tcheou-fou,* as three of the principal cities in China, and remarkable for the extent of their commerce and the advantageous trade they carry on.

There are two towers at *Sou-tcheou-fou*; one at the north, the other at the ſouth end. They are both alike, and in form and conſtruction reſemble that of *Cau-ming-tſi,* of which the reader has been ſo often reminded.

The ſuburbs are pretty large, and the veſſels which line the canal and quays innumerable. This is a ſure mark of proſperity and a flouriſhing trade. The city contains ſeveral triumphal arches of ſtone, the handſomeſt of which ſtands upon a quay exactly oppoſite to the place where our veſſels ſtopped. This triumphal arch was erected in honour of the Mandarin *Pong-hu-uun,* in the forty-third year of the reign of the Emperor *Kan hi* (grandfather to the preſent Emperor); that is to ſay, about the year 1702 of our era. It bears the following Chineſe inſcription:

THAT HE MAY BE REMEMBERED.

Theſe triumphal arches are called in China *Cap-pay-fong.*

On

On the other fide of the canal, in the fuburbs facing us, is a large fquare. Imperial building, with a double roof, and covered with yellow varnifhed tiles. In the middle of it ftands a ftone monument with an infcription. It is afflicting to fee that a want of care on the part of the adminiftration of the city has already fuffered feveral marks of decay to appear in this edifice.

We did not obferve any thing elfe worthy of remark; and found ourfelves ftrangely deceived in regard to this celebrated city.

I learned this evening from my Chinefe fervant, and was afterwards affured by our Interpreter, that we owe to our firft conductor all the difficulties that have been raifed in oppofition to our wifh of feeing the city in detail. He had concerted with the Mandarins the means of deceiving our hopes, particularly with refpect to a fight of the women, who are reckoned the handfomeft in all China, and who have fuch a reputation for gallantry throughout the Empire, that the court and the principal Mandarins procure from hence the ornaments of their feraglios. In order to attain his end with the greater certainty, he even went fo far as to poft up a prohibition before our arrival, forbidding any female to come in our way, under a fevere a severe penalty. It is no wonder then if our hopes were delusive.

With a conductor of a more generous nature we might have staid three days in the place, and have seen every thing worthy of attention as well as the environs; instead of which, our expectations were entirely frustrated by the base jealousy of this arrogant Mandarin, who did not however fail to purchase two pretty concubines, nor forget to carry them away with him.

This trade in women is a principal branch of the commerce of the city of *Sou-tcheou-fou*, and the best resource of many of its inhabitants, as well as those of *Hong-tcheou-fou*, in the province of *Tché-kiang*. *Sou-tcheou-fou*, however, bears away the palm from its rival. A great number of individuals have no other means of existence, and, with a view to this traffic, make excursions about the country, in order to buy of the poor inhabitants such of their children as promise to be beautiful.

They bring up these young girls with the greatest care, dress them elegantly, teach them all sorts of needlework, and to play upon different instruments of music, in order that their charms

charms and accomplifhments may render them agreeable to the perfons into whofe hands they may chance to fall.

The handfomeft of them are generally bought for the court and the Mandarins of the firft clafs. One who unites beauty with agreeable accomplifhments fetches from four hundred and fifty to feven hundred louis-d'ors, while there are fome who fell for lefs than a hundred.

The nature of the population in China affords two girls for a boy; a circumftance which admits of the fpeculations I am fpeaking of, and renders them highly beneficial.

From this general practice, as well as from the cuftom of giving a price, called a dowry, to the parents of the girl whom a man marries, a cuftom prevalent even among the firft perfonages of the Empire, it is evident that all the women in China are an article of trade.

The hufband, in certain cafes fpecified by the law, has a right to fell his lawful wife, unlefs her family choofe to take her back, and reftore the dowry they received at the time of her marriage.

There is no country in the world in which the women live in a greater ſtate of humiliation, or are leſs conſidered than in China. Thoſe whoſe huſbands are of high rank are always confined; thoſe of the ſecond claſs are a ſort of upper ſervants, deprived of all liberty; while thoſe of the lower are partakers with the men of the hardeſt kind of labour. If the latter become mothers it is an additional burthen, ſince while at work they carry the child tied upon the back, at leaſt till it is able to go alone.

Such is the fate of the Chineſe women; and, however hard it may appear to us, theſe weak beings ſuffer it with a patience and ſubmiſſion which habit alone can teach.

What a difference between their condition and that of the women in the greater part of Europe! Perhaps moroſe beings may be found to affirm, that there are ſome of the latter who would be benefited by participating for a time in the treatment the former endure.

It may be ſuppoſed, from what I have ſaid of the degradation of the fair ſex in China, that jealouſy is unknown there, and that the women might without danger have an intercourſe with

Euro-

Europeans; but the Chinese are not of that opinion; nor is there any one among them who would choose to risk an experiment, which they guard against, on the contrary, with the utmost vigilance.

Our stay at *Sou-tcheou-fou* having no longer an object, we quitted it at eight o'clock at night.

At about ten *li* from the city we passed by a very long stone bridge, called *Pau-tay-kian*, standing to the eastward of the canal. It has sixty-three arches, of which the three middle ones alone are arched, the others being covered with long flat stones laid across pillars. We travelled all night long.

22d. This morning at three o'clock our first Mandarin ordered the vessels to stop abreast of the city of *Uu-kiang-chen* till day-break, when we proceeded on our journey.

Uu-kiang-chen appears a moderately large place, and has extensive suburbs built alongside of the canal.

In the interior of the city is a tower of six stories high, which differs little in construction from

from that of *Cau-ming-tſi*, but is not in equally good repair.

At a small distance from the suburbs is a large stone bridge of five arches, kept in very good order. Each pier rests upon a single stone, in like manner as those of the bridge I mentioned yesterday. Near that I am now speaking of we passed through another, also of stone, the principal arch of which has a span of at least fifty feet, and is the largest I have hitherto seen.

Upwards of twenty *li* beyond the city of *Uu-kiang-chen* is a quay alongside of the canal, which has itself a facing of hewn stone on each side. The quay is interrupted or occupied by more than thirty stone bridges, almost all with arches. In the number are two of five, and another very handsome one of seven. The piers of these bridges, like those mentioned yesterday and to-day, rest upon masses of stone, each of a single block.

The quantity of hewn stone employed in such places only of this province as have lain upon our road is truly surprising, when we know that the nearest place from which it can be procured is a hundred and fifty *li* distant, and sometimes more.

more. These works must consequently have oc-ocasined enormous labour and expence.

The country we have passed through in this day's journey is lower than that of yesterday, and is divided by a number of little canals and ditches. Hence it is that little else than rice is cultivated. The ground continues to be uneven, and full of graves and trees, which produce a variety not disagreeable to the eye.

I remarked here a singular usage relative to the dead, whose coffins are deposited in any field indiscriminately, and upon the surface of the earth. Those who can afford it build a little square wall round the coffin, equal to it in height, over which a small roof is erected, covered with tiles; others lay straw and mats over it; while the lower class of people content themselves with laying merely a *stratum* of turf over the coffin, and leave it in that situation. We have passed by a great many graves of this kind during the two last days.

As the Chinese show a high degree of reverence for the dead, this mode of treating them, which appears so indecent, astonished me much. I enquired the reason, and was told that the land

land was so low, that the dead bodies could not be interred without lying in the water; an idea which the Chinese cannot bear, because they are persuaded that the deceased love a dry abode. After some time has elapsed, the coffins that have been thus left in the open fields are burnt with the bodies they contain; and the ashes are carefully collected, and put into covered urns, which are afterwards half buried in the earth. I saw several urns thus deposited by the road side.

This was the first time I had ever heard that the practice of burning the dead and collecting their ashes is customary in China, as it was among the ancient Greeks and Romans. I do not at least remember that in all I formerly read concerning China any thing like it is mentioned; nor had I ever heard of any thing of the kind in the thirty-six years I had been personally acquainted with the country; a space of time during which I frequently made enquiries of men of letters and information concerning every thing relative to the history, manners, and peculiarities of their native land. This fact is a convincing proof that there are very few Chinese who have a general knowledge of the whole Empire, or who are acquainted with the customs of the provinces they do not inhabit.

In

In the course of the morning we saw several fields sown with mustard already in flower. Upon higher ground situated along the canal we also saw plantations of young mulberry trees, intended to afford nourishment to silk-worms, which indicates that we are beginning to approach the manufactories of raw silk, which are principally carried on in the province of *Tché-kiang*, although that silk, as I have already said, very improperly bears the name of *Nam king*.

Since I have mentioned the guard-houses, or military posts of the other provinces, I shall here say, with respect to the province *Kiang-nam*, that they are all in very good condition, and sufficiently provided with troops, as we had it in our power to judge, since they did not fail to draw up under arms upon our road.

At a quarter past nine we passed by *Pat-chac-sau*, a very large place, and celebrated for its oil extracted from turnips, which are cultivated in great abundance. In this town we remarked a stone bridge of seven arches, the piers of which rested upon masses of stone of a single block.

Every day we pass by vessels laden with rice, which are going up the canal. Yesterday in
par-

particular, while we were at *Sou-tcheou fou,* the number that went by was incredible.

The ground has assumed a level surface, and, as every thing is planted in beds, the fields have the appearance of kitchen gardens. Even the very mulberry trees, whose growth appears to be stopped at man's height, are also planted in beds. It is highly probable that this district is subject to heavy rains, which require this precaution, in order to carry off the water more speedily, and to preserve the land from damage.

At eleven o'clock we were opposite a little lake, situated to the westward, and only separated from us by a quay, similar to those of which I have already spoken.

At noon we passed *Phing-mong-chan,* a large and populous place, and so well built, that it would be disgraced by a comparison with many cities. It contains five stone bridges, one of which has three arches, and two have only one; but they are of fifty or sixty feet diameter. These are at the end of the place, and kept in very good order.

The

The piers here alfo ftand upon fingle blocks of ftone. In the two great arches which I have juft mentioned the vault or curve is formed of eleven ftones, and fix compofe the width of the bridge. Ten of the ftones of the vault are each eight feet long, as well as I was able to judge from the height of a man, who was ftanding upon one of the blocks at the foot of the piers, and who ferved me as a meafure. The key-ftone is fix feet broad. The arch in its whole fweep defcribes a line fomewhat eliptic, the curve being fmaller than that of a femi-circle.

The laft bridge, at the end of *Phing-mong-chan*, has ten great ftones in the vault, and that which ferves as the key-ftone is fmaller than in the preceding one. There are alfo eight fmaller ftones, each a foot broad, let into the larger ones. All the latter have a groove, which defcribes throughout the whole of them a portion of an elipfis correfponding with the edge of the arch, and the line formed by the meeting of two ftones is in the direction of a radius drawn to the centre of the elipfis to which the curve of the arch belongs. In a word, the whole is a proof that the ftricteft geometrical rules have been obferved in the conftruction of this bridge.

This

This place contains several temples of moderate size, which are kept in very good order. One of them is dedicated to *Kiam-long-citay-onan*, one to *Sam-coun-tong*, and two to *Sing-ouon*.

At *Phing-mong-chan* a great trade appears to be carried on in bamboos, which grow there in remarkable abundance.

Having passed this place, we found ourselves shortly after abreast of a great lake, in the centre of which is a little tabular island, with a pagoda standing upon it, dedicated to *Fat-lou*.

At half past one we came to a very rich and extensive village, situated west of the canal, where, as we were told, there is a considerable manufactory of satin and other stuffs of silk. The houses are, for the most part, large, and well arranged. This village is called *Ouon-ca-tché*.

At half past three we reached *Ouon-con-can*, the first place we met with after entering the province of *Tché-kiang*; here our conductor ordered a halt. The village is of some extent, and at its north end is a large and handsome triumphal arch of stone, near which stands a small but neat pagoda. Beyond the village are two stone bridges,

bridges, near to each other, one of which has three arches, the other only one. The centre arch of the firſt bridge, as well as I was able to judge by the ſtones which formed the vault, was fixty-four feet in width. One of the ſide arches is much ſunk, but ſtill appears to be ſufficiently ſtrong to laſt many years: an advantage which hewn ſtone poſſeſſes in a high degree over bricks; for the latter yields upon the ſlighteſt ſhock; all connexion is diſſolved, and total ruin enſues. The houſes of the village all appear to be kept in good order. The inhabitants procure their means of ſubſiſtence from the manufacture of ſilk. This is the moſt noted place in the Empire for making copper baſons, or *gomgoms*, an inſtrument which the Chineſe beat upon in ſaluting any one, to whom they wiſh to pay particular honour.

Between two houſes ſituated alongſide of the canal, are four great triumphal arches, which indicate that ſeveral perſons of great celebrity muſt have been inhabitants of this place.

After having taken a repaſt we ſet off at half paſt ſix. As far as *Ouon-ca-tchi* the wind was in our favour.

23d. We arrived before three o'clock in the morning at a village called *Ca-hong-hou*, where

VOL. II.   O   we

we changed our trackers and fet off again two hours after, directing our courfe to the fouth-weft.

At day-break I obferved that the furface of the country was become uneven. We paffed by a great many hills covered with trees, among which we diftinguifhed whole plantations of mulberry trees, and a great number of orchards. There was very little arable land. The number of trees and fhrubs with which we were furrounded, confined our view to a fmall diftance on each fide of the canal. The few houfes that I was able to fee between them, were long and well built. Thefe circumftances again announce the rearing of filk-worms, which require a great deal of room.

In anfwer to my queftions, I was told that the mulberry-tree cultivated here, is of the kind which bears the dark purple-coloured fruit, of a very agreeable tafte. Hence it fhould feem that the filk-worm is here fed with the leaves of our well-known domeftic mulberry tree, and not with that of the wild one.

In France and Italy it is affirmed that the latter is alone fit for the nourifhment of this infect, and that the leaves of the common mulberry tree are

too

too coarse, and too little suited to the nature of the animal for those that are fed upon it, to produce silk of a good quality. But the raw silk of *Tché-kiang* being reckoned the finest and most valuable in the known world, we may conclude that the European opinion concerning the mulberry-tree is rather a prejudice than the result of decisive experience.

I will even venture to give implicit belief to what I have been told in this respect by those whom I have consulted, because they are so well acquainted with the nature of the mulberry tree, that they afterwards observed to me, that the female tree alone produces the fruit, while the male bears nothing but flowers, without any fructification. I was even much astonished to hear these distinctions made by one of the common people, whose business was navigation, and not agriculture. As he also described to me the fruit, its taste, and its colour with wonderful accuracy, I had no room left for doubt, especially as the trees of which I had a very near view, appeared to me precisely the same as our garden mulberry trees in Holland, and exceedingly different from the wild mulberry tree (*murier rose*). The latter appears unknown in this country.

At a quarter paſt nine we paſſed through a bridge called *Cha-ong-kiou,* near which are ſeveral ſhops by the ſide of the canal. The bridge is ſtrong and well conſtructed. From the dimenſions of the ſtones I was led to eſtimate the circumference of its ſemi-circular arch at twenty ſix feet, and its diameter at more than fifty-ſeven*. I obſerved of this bridge, as I had already done of ſeveral others, that between the large ſtones, ſmaller ones had been inſerted: theſe are alſo of a ſingle block, and the width of the bridge ſerves as a meaſure for their length. Thus, the arch that I am juſt ſpeaking of, is compoſed of only ſeventy-ſix ſtones; viz. ſixty-ſix great ſtones placed in eleven rows, which are ſeparated by the ten intermediate ones: they are all at leaſt half a foot thick. Over theſe there is another layer of ſtones, placed horizontally, each of which is ſomething more than three inches thick. All theſe ſtones are a kind of grey granite, and exceedingly hard. The width of the road-way is generally nine or ten French feet.

* Here appears to be ſome miſtake. At leaſt if the tranſlation render correctly the ſenſe of theſe words of the text: *Les dimenſions des pierres m'ont fait donner au contour de ſon arche demi-ſphérique vingt-ſin pieds et plus de cinquante ſept pieds à ſon diametre.*

Near

Near this bridge are feven triumphal arches of ftone; fix ftanding three and three, on two different fpots: the feventh alone. They are dedicated for the moft part to women; for inftance, to three very young widows, who refufed to marry again; and to an old woman of ninety-eight years of age. A man celebrated for filial piety has alfo obtained one. The infcription engraved on the pedeftal of the other being concealed by a hut, we could not difcover the motive of its erection.

In proportion as we advanced, and new fpace was difclofed to our view, we perceived the number of mulberry trees increafe; and towards noon the country was entirely covered with them.

A few minutes before twelve o'clock we paffed by one of the Emperor's feats called *Chap-moun-ouan-ouoncong*, entirely furrounded with walls. The roofs are in a very neglected ftate, and nothing has a pleafing appearance except a ftone quay, built upon the fpot fronting the Imperial houfe, and appearing to have recently had a thorough repair. The Emperor not having travelled for the laft twelve years to the fouthern parts of the Empire, it appears that all the money is referved for his prefent country refidencies; or perhaps fome of it goes to fill the pockets of individuals.

viduals. Formerly the Monarch went as far as *Hong-tcheou-fou* to divert himself in these countries, and to give a look to the southern provinces, by which they were sure to be benefited. Then the Mandarins took care that every thing should appear in good condition. The roads, the bridges, the quays, the edifices and summer palaces of the Emperor, every thing was at all times ready to undergo his examination. These constant repairs were also extended to a great number of public buildings Here, as in Europe, and every where else, the eye of the master is often necessary, its influence generally conducing to the happiness of the people, and the good order of the state.

At noon we were a-breast of *Chap-moun-san*, which stands on both banks. We were half an hour in passing through as much of the canal as corresponds with its length. It appears at a distance very closely built, and very populous, as was attested by the number of persons, both male and female, who thronged to see us, composing crowds at which we were perfectly astonished.

Chap-moun-san must carry on a great trade in young plants or sets of the mulberry tree, since I

saw

faw heaps of them putting on board boats from one end of the canal to the other.

I alfo faw feveral veffels pafs by loaded with indigo, in their way to *Sou-tcheou fou*, where it is ufed in dying ·filk and linen. This fubftance is cultivated and manufactured in the diftrict of *Tay-chiou-fou*, in the province of *Tché-kiang*. The Chinefe, however, do not keep it as elfewhere in dry pieces or cakes, but leave it in a moift ftate refembling wet clay, and carry it in bafkets to the places where the dyers and manufacturers refide. The ufe of that dye being very general in China for all kinds of ftuffs and linen, the confumption is confiderable. All the indigo manufactured in China remains in the country; for I never had the leaft reafon to fuppofe that any was exported to Europe, which its moift ftate would indeed render impracticable. The province of *Quang-tong* produces a great quantity of that colouring matter.

At half paft one, we paffed by a place which appeared to me to be a common burying ground. In one of the angles were feveral coffins, placed near one another on the ground; and a little farther on, funeral urns half buried in the earth. A little farther ftill in the fame piece of ground, are three handsome hexagonal columns of stone, standing by the side of each other: they are ten or twelve feet high. The middle one, which exceeds the others in size, may be four or five feet in diameter. A single convex stone, of small thickness, serves as a capital to each of them, and from it's middle proceeds a double ball of metal chafed. In the front of these columns, which stand under the shade of a lofty tree, an inscription is engraved. I was assured that funereal urns were lodged inside of them.

By the side of those columns is an antique tomb, which, to judge from its dimensions, must contain two coffins; and which, according to the indications afforded by the growth of ivy, and by the effect of time upon the stones, must have stood at least two hundred years.

Near this tomb is a pagoda in which the dead are deposited previously to their interment, and where an offering is made in their favour. I took a sketch of this spot, in order to have a correct drawing made of it at Canton.

At half past two we came to another burying ground, on which stand four stone columns, intended to contain sepulchral urns. These co‑
lumns

lumns may be about fix feet fquare, and ten or twelve feet high, with capitals of more or lefs elevation.

At the entrance of this cemetery, which is fituated to the weftward of the canal, while that of the preceding one is to the eaftward, are four triumphal arches of ftone; but one of them is fallen to the ground.

At three o'clock we came to the fuburbs of *Che-men-chen,* which are pretty extenfive, and then to the city itfelf. Its ramparts bear all the marks of antiquity. They are of hewn ftone as high as the parapet, which, as well as the embrafures, is of brick. But the whole of it is at prefent in a ruinous ftate. According to the line we defcribed while paffing by the city, it is of an irregular form approaching a fquare. It is faid to be twenty *li* in circumference; to be well built, and to be inhabited by many perfons of opulence and diftinction.

At the entrance of the fuburbs we paffed by a confiderable convent, with its temple and dependencies. The temple is dedicated to the Chriftian *Kiam-long-citay-ouang,* whom I have feveral times had occafion to mention. We perceived in the suburbs and city of *Che-men-chen*, two or three other convents of mean appearance.

Being come to the south side of the city, our first conductor ordered a halt, an opportunity of which we availed ourselves to take our repast. We were then in front of a noble building, which when the Emperor used to travel to the south, served him as lodgings on his passage through this place. It is called *Ouan-cong*, and appears to be kept in very good order.

At a quarter past six we set off again, our direction, which in the morning had changed to the south, having turned again to the south-west.

The country, like that we travelled through yesterday, is interfected with canals and ditches. We passed through nine great bridges, (besides those which I have particularly mentioned under this day's date) and through several small ones, all of stone, and almost all constructed like those I have so amply described: I took a regular plan of them.

We saw besides thirteen triumphal arches, two of the most remarkable of which owed their erection to the exemplary conduct of two sons towards

towards their parents. Almoft all the reft were in honour of faithful wives, or girls who died virgins. Three others were lying in ruins. We have then feen in the courfe of this day no lefs than twenty-feven of thefe pieces of architecture, erected to different virtues, and giving real celebrity to the places where they ftand. Whenever I faw thefe figns of public refpect for virtuous beings, I felt a fort of confufion and fecret pain, upon thinking that among us there exift no fuch marks of a juft homage paid to valuable qualities, and calculated to excite emulation.

Is conduct, or an action, in itfelf worthy of praife, to be lefs commended becaufe it belongs to an obfcure individual, than if it could be attributed to a perfon of high rank, who has been taught by his education to fet a juft value upon true honour? As to me, I profefs the contrary opinion, exactly becaufe elevated rank furnifhes an incitement which is wanting to him, whofe neglected education has neither afforded him great models, nor ufeful leffons.

24th. At half paft three in the morning we paffed under a confiderable bridge of three arches, the middle one being of very confiderable dimenfions. The canal is become wider, and our route, which

which during a part of the night had taken a direction weftward, has turned again to the fouth.

A little after four we paffed a large place called *Thong-ci-fan,* where a number of handfome houfes are built along the canal, and where there is a *conquan,* or occafional refidence for the Emperor. At the fouth end of this place ftands a beautiful triumphal arch of ftone, of confiderable fize, and ornamented with a great deal of fculpture and gilding.

At fun-rife we perceived mountains at a great diftance, extending from the eaft to the fouth, and fome alfo in a weftern direction.

The country was higher on the weftern than on the eaftern fide of the canal. The latter for this reafon grows fewer mulberry trees, which require a high fituation. Corn and other vegetables are fown in beds of only a foot and a half wide, as tobacco is planted in Holland, with little ditches or drains between them. The earth taken from thefe ditches ferves to raife the beds, and preferve the feed from the ravages committed by heavy rains.

In

In front of the road, or rather quay, and by the fide of the canal, runs a wall of hewn ftone, which fuffered greatly in feveral places by the inundation of laft year, on account of its bad foundation, confifting of nothing but two rows of thin piles. Immediately on thefe reft the lower ftones, without any other fupport, even that of a plank. The earth being wafhed away by the water, the piles can no longer fupport the weight of the ftones, which are each about fifteen inches cube, and are piled upon one another to the height of eight or ten feet: they confequently fink in, or give way, and the mafonry tumbles to pieces.

After confidering attentively the folidity and excellent execution of the bridges, I was greatly aftonifhed at finding ftructures in the fame places befpeaking the groffeft ignorance, and even ftupidity. This long quay is neverthelefs equally neceffary with the bridges, and requires to be kept in as good repair.

At eight o'clock the country to the eaftward grew higher, and the orchards of mulberry trees began in confequence to re-appear. On both fides of the canal was alfo a confiderable number of peach trees in bloffom, which made the profpect

pect very agreeable. I am affured that peaches are very common here, and much larger than in Europe. I faw alfo a great number of China orange, plum, and other kinds of fruit trees.

At eight o'clock we were in fight of a very high infulated mountain, ftanding between two branches of the canal, at about five *li* diftance to the eaftward. It is covered with a variety of trees to the very fummit, on which are built, under a thick fhade, a convent and a pagoda called *Ling-phin-chan*. All the other mountains were bare, and without the fmalleft verdant fpot.

The guard-houfes of this province by which we have paffed are all in good condition, and appear to have their complement of ten foldiers, with an officer of the gilt button. Thefe military pofts are in this province at unequal diftances from each other, from five to ten *li*, according as the diftrict is more or lefs populous. On our prefent road they are only feparated by an interval of five *li*.

During the morning we paffed by feveral cemeteries, interfperfed with noble ftone columns, infide of which are funeral urns. We alfo paffed by a dozen of convents and temples, for

the

the moſt part in good preſervation; but we did not perceive a ſingle triumphal arch.

At eleven o'clock we found ourſelves under a large bridge of three arches, ſimilar to that we had ſeen in the morning. After paſſing this bridge we came to the ſuburbs of the celebrated city of *Hong-tcheou-fou*. They are interſected by ſeveral ditches with handſome bridges acroſs them, under ſeveral of which we paſſed. At three quarters paſt twelve we came to the place where veſſels ſtop, and where there is a large and handſome edifice, intended to ſerve as lodgings for the principal Mandarins, when they travel.

Shortly after our third conductor came to inform the Ambaſſador and me that an Imperial entertainment will be given us to-morrow in the city. He requeſted us to hold ourſelves in readineſs at an early hour, becauſe it is intended to ſhew us ſeveral things worthy of attention. In conſequence of this he propoſed to us not to dine at the place of the ceremony; but to defer that repaſt till the evening, when we are to embark on board of other boats, into which our baggage will be removed during our excurſion. We acquieſced in every thing without the leaſt oppoſition.

fition. He added that we are to ftop again near this place the day after to-morrow in our new veffels, in order that we may, if we think proper, procure a few curiofities, or a fight of any thing interefting, which gives us much pleafure; for we have heard *Hong-tcheou-fou* and its environs fo highly extolled, that our curiofity is ftrongly excited, and we fhall be very happy to gratify it.

This afternoon our five gentlemen went into the city to fee if the fhops contained any thing remarkable; and returned at three o'clock without having obferved any thing worthy of notice. They were not able to proceed far into the city, the gates being a great diftance from our anchoring place. They confequently faw little more than the fuburbs.

The change of veffels, which is to take place to-morrow, will not be advantageous to us as to accommodations, thofe we are to go on board of being fmaller than thofe we are to leave, on account of the fhoals that obftruct the reft of the river. Our baggage is to be conveyed thirty *li* by land, as far as the little town of *Tak-hau*, where thofe veffels are waiting for us, in confequence of there being no communication between the river and the canal along which we have hitherto travelled. This removal is as un-

pleafant

pleafant as troublefome, becaufe our effects are always fure to fuftain confiderable injury. Fortunate will it be if fair weather permit our *Coulis* to go the whole diftance without ftopping!

25th. We got our baggage ready at an early hour of the morning, in order that it may be conveyed to the veffels, which are to carry us to the confines of this province.

The hire of our prefent *yachts* from *Von-ca-fen* hither is only nine Louis d'ors; a very fmall fum, efpecially if we confider that from twelve to fixteen men are employed on board of them. The Mandarins do thefe poor wretches great injuftice, in order to fill their own pockets, the Emperor's name ferving as a cover for plunder.

Each cart employed in carrying our baggage from *Pe-king* to *Von-ca-fen*, had only two Louis d'ors for a route of twenty-three days, although there were five horfes and three men to each. Luckily they found a profitable load to carry back with them; for in general they are obliged to go as far as the province of *Kiang-nam*, without earning any thing whatever. The expence of their return will not however be forgotten to be inferted in the account. Our conductors, and all their fervants,

fervants, know well how much fuch fortunate chances ought to bring them.

At eight o'clock the Ambaffador and I were requefted to repair to the city with our whole fuite; we accordingly went in ftate in our palanquins. At three quarters paft two we entered a building by the fide of the Imperial palace, whence, after waiting half an hour, we were conducted on foot to the latter place. There we were received as at *Sou-tcheou-fou* with the greateft ceremony. The garrifon was under arms; and two Mandarins led us to the hall where the Emperor's *chap* was laid upon an altar. The *Fou-yuen* of the city and province, who is coufin to the Emperor, and who wears the pale-coloured button and peacock's feather in his cap, was on the right hand of the altar, while a great number of principal Mandarins ftood on each fide at fome diftance behind. When pretty near the altar we ftopped: the *Fou-yuen* then came in front of it, and performed the falute of honour: rifing again, he took the Emperor's letter, which was upon the altar, and advanced towards us. At this moment we knelt down, and he communicated to us through the medium of the *Lingua* what he feemed to read in the letter, " that his Imperial Majefty, fatisfied to the laft
" degree

"degree with the Dutch Embaſſy, as well as
"with the conduct of the Ambaſſador and his
"ſuite, had given orders to entertain his Excel-
"lency in his name, to make him preſents, to
"treat him in the kindeſt manner, and to ſhew
"him the moſt remarkable things the city con-
"tained," &c. &c.

The letter being peruſed, we performed the
ſalute of honour, and then roſe and preſented our
reſpects to the *Fou-yuen* and ſome of the principal
Mandarins, who begged us to ſeat ourſelves upon
cuſhions, in order to ſee the play. Little tables
were afterwards ſet before us, covered with ſweetmeats and fruit, that were removed to make
room for porringers full of hot viands, which in
their turn were ſucceeded by roaſt and boiled
meat. Theſe we did not even taſte.

During this repaſt, actors and tumblers, richly
and variouſly habited, diſplayed their talents upon
a ſuperb theatre oppoſite the hall. This diver-
ſion engaged our attention for half an hour: we
then roſe to go and ſee the intereſting things, the
idea of which had ſtrongly excited our curioſity.

The preſents were brought and put upon tables
in the hall. The *Fou-yuen* offered them to us,
and

and we expreffed our gratitude by a new falute of honour. This ceremony being at an end, the *Fou-yuen* advanced towards the Ambaffador, and told him in the moft affable manner, that in conformity with the Emperor's orders, he had directed two Mandarins to fhew us fome curious objects worthy of our attention. His Excellency having thanked him both for the favour and his kindnefs, we took our leave. It was eleven o'clock when we left the palace to make our excurfion.

I fhall begin my defcription by the city:

Hong-tcheou-fou is fixty *li* in circumference (fix leagues). It is of irregular form; in fome places the walls are circular; in others ftraight; and in others again, they wind up the fide of lofty mountains. The interior of the city is pretty well built, and contains feveral handfome houfes. It is interfected by a number of ditches: the ftreets are not wide, but they are well paved with large hewn ftones. In paffing through them I remarked fome capital fhops difplaying a great choice of goods, and warehoufes containing all forts of merchandife. Among others, to my great aftonifhment, I faw three watch-maker's fhops, and a great number of others full of fmoaked hams.

hams. It looked as if Weſtphalia was in China, and in the vicinity of this city.

I obſerved alſo ſeveral very pretty triumphal arches of ſtone, and two of remarkable ſize and grandeur, ſtanding cloſe by the ſide of each other, and within the city gates. Near theſe gates two pieces of cannon are planted, carrying a ball of about ſix pounds weight, and mounted upon carriages with three wheels.

In one of the ſtreets I alſo remarked a Mahometan moſque.

On the architrave of the building is an inſcription in Arabic, of which I took a copy.

On this ſubject our third conductor aſſured me that *Sou-tcheou-fou*, and ſome other city contained moſques likewiſe, but that the Emperor having made war twelve years ago againſt a Mahometan nation upon the weſtern frontier of the Empire, had baniſhed all foreigners of that ſect from thoſe three places, ſo that there are no longer any to be found in China.

Having reached the outſide of the city, we had a good opportunity of ſeeing the walls, which

which are of great antiquity; they are conſtructed of hewn ſtone as high as the parapet, and are of brick-work above. Its whole ſurface is covered with different paraſitical plants, and even with ſmall ſhrubs, which have found means to grow in the crevices of the walls.

We were carried to a conſiderable diſtance along the weſt ſide of the city without the walls, till we perceived the lake of *Tſay-von-cang*, ſo famous throughout China, on account of the Emperor's ſummer palaces, which ſtand upon its borders, and in its vicinity. This lake is ſituated between the eaſtern part of the city, and high mountains, interſperſed with pines and other kinds of trees, and winding from the north-weſt end of the city, to the ſouth-weſt of it, at which part the walls are carried over the top of one of them. On the ſummit of the others, are five convents or pagodas, viz. *Pac-chan-hong*, *Samſing-ying*, *Samſing-chec*, *Nam-chan-hong*, and *Ouang-tſi*, all ſtanding under the ſhade of lofty trees.

The lake contains three iſlands, of which the moſt northerly, and alſo the largeſt, called *Ouong-cong-chan*, has a mountain in the middle. The centre iſland is called *Lok-yet-chung*, and the ſouthern one *Tong-tſan-tſi*. Several villas ſtand upon

upon each of them, and to thefe the Emperor was in the habit of going to amufe himfelf every day while at *Hong-tcheou-fou.*

Two roads are carried over the lakes. They are paved in the middle, and on their fides are planted with willows, bananas, peach, and other fruit trees. There are alfo a great many ftone bridges of a fingle arch, in order that the little pleafure boats may pafs to both fides of thefe roads. On each of the bridges formerly ftood open pavilions, feveral of which are now lying in ruins upon the ground.

One of the two roads leads from the city to the great ifland, to the north of which is a noble ftone bridge of five arches, ferving as a communication between the ifland and the main. The other road which paffes over the weftern part of the lake lies north and fouth.

We were carried along the foot of the mountains to the north of the lake, a little diftance from the city. On the fummit of thofe mountains we were fhewn a tower, called *Pau-foc-thafe*, which muft, when entire, have refembled that of *Cau-ming-tfi*, and others of the fame kind; but nothing now remains except the mafs of building,

ing, and the beautiful fpire of caft metal, with chains ftill hanging about it. The roof, as well as the galleries, which were of wood, are either deftroyed by the confuming hand of time, or perhaps by the action of celeftial fire. In going along the mountains we alfo paffed near a great convent, the neighbourhood of which contains feveral handfome temples. It is called *Tay-faa-tfi*, and makes a very fine appearance. At the foot of thefe mountains, as alfo in feveral places a fmall way up their fides, are a confiderable number of little low buildings, in every one of which are coffins containing dead bodies, to be kept there till the time of their interment. Thefe little buildings are divided into fifteen or twenty cells, all following one another, and calculated to receive a coffin each. The whole circumference of the lake being almoft entirely full of them, it may be fafely faid that the dead bodies lie there by hundreds, and that fome of them have been waiting to be inhumed for thefe fixty or eighty years, or perhaps more. Thefe places, and the depofits made there, are under the fafe-guard of the bonzes belonging to the neighbouring convents, who receive on that account a remuneration which contributes in a great degree to their fupport.

Further

Further on we found three or four hamlets, full of shops; and several triumphal arches of stone, standing either between the houses or near the sepulchres.

When we came to an elbow made by the mountains to the north-west, we were desired to alight from our palanquins, in order to see the tomb of the celebrated *Calao*, named *Ngok-fi*, or otherwise *Ngok-fo-hand-kan*, whose story I related under the date of the 19th of this month. The tomb of this unfortunate, but estimable man, consists of a hemisphere of brick. On the left of it is another smaller one, which covers the remains of *Ngok-ouang*, his son. In front of the great tomb, and opposite the middle of it, is an altar supporting a vase for incense; the whole of hewn stone, and intended for sacrifices offered to the memory of this noble character.

The two tombs constructed upon an elevated spot, are separated by a wall with a triple gate, from a large square fore-court, along the middle of which, in a line from the first outer gate to the inner one, stand a number of antique figures cut in stone, and opposite to each other. Each row consists of three Mandarins, a horse saddled, a ram lying down, and a sitting lion. On the two sides fides of the firſt outer gate are alſo the bronze ſtatues of the four calumniators, placed two by two on their knees, with their hands tied behind their back; their faces turned towards the ſepulchre; their eyes caſt down, and their names inſcribed upon their breaſt, viz. *Then-kouey* and *Ouong-tſi* his wife; then *Mau-tché-lu* and *Loua-u-tchit*. For more than two centuries, it has been an eſtabliſhed cuſtom among the Chineſe, when they go to offer ſacrifices before the tomb, to ſtrike with a bit of ſtone or wood upon the forehead of the ſtatues of theſe four villains, as a ſign of horror at their crime. At the time of our viſit, one of them was detached from its pedeſtal, and lying in a corner near the gate.

The whole ſepulchre is ſurrounded with walls, and a number of trees are ſtanding by it. A large and ſuperb gate, with three paſſages, forms the entrance, which leads into a great court paved with hewn ſtone, and having on each ſide two beautiful cylindrical columns, alſo of hewn ſtone, and about fifteen feet high. A little further on are two plain ſquare pillars, of the ſame height as the columns.

After having viewed this juſtly celebrated monument, to which time ſeems to have added
ſomething

something still more august, by bringing round eight hundred annual revolutions of the sun, since the moment, when in remembrance of an involuntary but fatal error, the Emperor ordered it to be erected, to vindicate in an authentic manner the memory of that virtuous Minister of State; after having viewed this monument, I say, we were conducted to the south side of the lake; thence we were carried over the embankment or road which runs along the west side of the lake, and of which I have already spoken, in order to see the Imperial palace, and other things worthy of notice.

I there got out of my palanquin to walk, and be the better able to make observations.

I then examined the island of *Ou-ou-cong* to the west and south, having already seen the two other sides of it. In this quarter it is planted with trees up to the very summit, having also a great number of handsome habitations standing among them.

To the south are buildings belonging to the Emperor, which, together with the gardens, form a very pleasing view. To the north and east are much fewer dwellings; but a mixture

of

of small houses or receptacles for coffins, and the tombs there, compose a landscape no doubt less rich, but calculated to impress the man of sensibility, and to occupy his mind with ideas truly philosophic.

To the westward of the road along which we were going, I passed by two of the Emperor's summer palaces, both situated upon two peninsulas, and surrounded with trees and flower gardens. At the end of this road, and near the foot of the mountain, we were conducted to his principal residence, called *Ce-ou-yau-tien-nan*, situated in a hollow of the mountain, and consisting of several detached edifices, built upon rocks upon different parts of the declivity.

Almost every thing in this picturesque situation is entirely the work of nature; and if she has sometimes borrowed the assistance of art, the efforts of the latter have been so happy, that it seems still as if nature has been working alone: this delightful variety produces a fascinating prospect. From the pavilions and domes placed here and there upon the declivity of the mountain, the eye commands a full view of the lake, and of the islands it contains; and on the other side, takes in the different buildings, convents, tombs,

and

and towers, which are scattered upon the flanks of other mountains, and which embellish their summits. So many objects united, compose the most attractive scene the imagination can conceive.

Being at a sufficient elevation, we had a complete view of the two flat islands in the lake; one of them, called *Tong-tsau-tsi*, contains two large ponds. In the front of this island, we remarked three pillars of cast iron, standing in the water in a triangular position. The part of these pillars or columns which appears above water, terminates in a cone. I was told that they are about eighteen feet high, seven feet diameter at their base, and have already been standing eight hundred years.

This renders it still more painful to see that in general these summer palaces bear so many marks of negligence, and of the decay which is the natural consequence of it. It is the effect of the Emperor's absence for the last twelve years, and of a belief that his great age opposes an invincible obstacle to his return. These places, when kept in good order, must have been in the summer season a kind of terrestrial paradise; an asylum where every thing invited to pleasure and sensuality. It is not without reason that this lake and

its

its environs are so renowned throughout the whole Chinese Empire; and most assuredly if nature had created such happy situations in Europe, their beauties would be incessantly proclaimed.

It is impossible for me to give a more exact description, after a short, and in some degree a superficial examination. It would require eight days, perhaps even double the time, to see and to admire all the beauties of the place, and to investigate every thing attentively, so as to let neither situation, edifice, island, nor prospect escape; and after all it would be impossible to avoid overlooking something or other.

Nevertheless, to please my own taste, and to gratify my reader, whose curiosity must be excited by my imperfect description, I borrowed from *Duhalde* a plan of the lake and city, and afterwards augmented and corrected it according to my own personal observations; and by these means an idea may be formed of the enchanting situation of each of those imperial villas.

After having been entertained by our conductors in one of the halls with refreshments consisting of fruits, pastry, and a dish of tea, we quitted this delightful spot, to go and see a very celebrated

celebrated convent and temple, which ftand at no great diftance.

The principal bonze came out to meet us in the forecourt, and accompanied us, in order to point out what was worthy of our notice. Every thing is in very good order, and the principal halls of the temple are both magnificent and fpacious. In a large fquare lateral building, having a circular gallery with two long galleries opening into it, and interfecting each other at right angles in the centre, are placed five hundred images of Saints, nearly as large as life, and fitting in different poftures. Some of them are painted and varnifhed, but for the moft part they are gilt all over.

We were defired to obferve that the Emperor *Kien-long* is already included in the number of Saints, although ftill living; a proof of adulation greater than that infpired by the chiefs of other nations, and fuch as a wife Prince ought to reject; but fince the Emperor of China is in the habit of being ferved and honoured like a god, it is very natural that he fhould let himfelf be inferted in the lift of the beatified before his death.

All

All thefe figures of Saints are difpofed in fuch a manner that there is a row feated along the walls on both fides of the galleries, while in the middle two are placed ftanding back to back, fo that it requires a confiderable time to fee them all. The trouble, however, is not to be regretted on account of the variety of the figures and poftures that prefent themfelves to the fpectator, while turning continually between the different rows, which form altogether a kind of labyrinth.

Some of the principal ftatues which occupy the centre are of bronze, as well as feveral antique cenfers and other facred veffels. We were afterwards conducted to a little apartment near a well, the depth of which I eftimated at more than thirty feet. A lighted candle was let down into it by means of a cord, to enable us to diftinguifh a tree ftanding in the water at the bottom. This tree, or rather this ftump, which has been fawed off horizontally, is more than a foot in diameter. The Chinefe related to us with the greateft folemnity, and with an air of conviction, that this tree continued conftantly to grow from the bottom of the well till it had furnifhed exactly as much wood as was wanting for the conftruction of the convent and temples; after which it remained in its prefent ftate. It is more eafy

to

to relate this miracle than to prevail upon Europeans to believe it in this enlightened age; but the Chinese have not the least doubt of its reality, their superstition being in all respects equal to that of the Portuguese for the blessed Saint Anthony of Padua.

After having seen every thing in this convent, the residence of at least three hundred bonzes, we took leave of their chief who attended us as far as the outer court. At a small distance from thence, we came to the ruins of the tower of *Lau-y-hong-thap*, which is supposed to have stood fifteen hundred years. It is nothing more than a mass of building, of which the seven stories still exist; but of which all the wooden-work, such as galleries, balconies, projecting roofs and ornaments, which were probably of the same kind as those of *Cau-ming-tsi*, have been entirely destroyed or consumed by lightning.

This long period of time is no doubt the cause of the stones being honey-combed all over; there are even places where large pieces are wanting, which appear to have been broken off; but what remains of this building is still sufficient to preserve its name and its remembrance for several centuries to come.

Vol. II. Q The

The origin of this tower has been made the subject of a dramatic piece, which I saw represented several times at Canton; but the plot is too complicated, and the ground-work too fabulous, for me to feel the smallest inclination to give an account of it, especially as it is not calculated to please Europeans.

I measured the external part of the tower, and found that one of the sides of the octagon is equal to forty-two French feet, so that its total circumference must be three hundred and thirty-six. Millions of bricks must have been employed in the construction of this building, the height of which may be estimated at a hundred and eighty feet, according to what I shall say hereafter of a similar tower.

Going a considerable way up a mountain at some distance from the tower, we came to a pavilion, under which we found a long and very ancient inscription. From this elevation the prospect is still more extensive than from the summer-palace of which I have already spoken. Hence we could discover the whole of the city, which enabled us to judge of its form, of the style of its buildings, and of its immense extent. The reader may therefore confidently rely upon all I have said upon the subject.

As

As it was about three o'clock in the afternoon, we refolved to put an end to our excurfion, and to go on board our new veffels. Extremely well pleafed with all that had been fhewn us, we thanked our conductors, took leave of them, and again got into our palanquins.

Near this fpot we paffed through a very populous place, and afterwards through a valley lying between two mountains fituated near the fouth-weft angle of *Hong-tcheou-fou*. While going along this piece of road, which is for the moft part paved with hewn ftone, we met with a convent and feveral habitations.

As foon as we came in fight of the fouth-weft gate, the garrifon drew up under arms on both fides of the road, and founded their conchs while we were paffing through the ranks. This garrifon was compofed of feveral corps varioufly clothed and armed; fome with bows and arrows, the others with mufkets. The latter have pikes, and the former fwords and bucklers; while others carry cutlaffes at the end of long ftaves. Each corps has alfo its particular colours, red, crimfon, white, green, and blue. Both foldiers and officers are well appointed, and make a very martial appearance. The foldiers all wear polifhed and

fhining

shining helmets. At each end of the line the Ambassador was saluted with three guns.

At four o'clock we reached the town of *Tsak-hau*, at the entrance of which were troops drawn up like those I have just mentioned. Here also the Ambassador was twice saluted. This place, which is pretty large, contains a number of good houses, and a slender tower of seven stories.

After leaving it we came to the residence of the *Hou-pou*, or Custom-house, a handsome building of considerable size, at some distance from which we perceived our vessels upon the river. The intermediate ground between it and the custom-house is unsound, and is covered with a kind of mud or slime deposited by the water. It is over this space that four-wheel carts, drawn by buffaloes, carry every thing that is to be embarked.

Tsak-hau is the place where all the vessels bring up that are laden with merchandize for *Hong-tcheou-fou*, or intended to take on board what is sent from that city.

In order to facilitate the passage to our vessels, the Chinese took all the carriages, more than two hundred

hundred in number, and by ranging them in a line one after another, made as it were two bridges, by means of which happy invention we were carried to the veſſels, as well as our baggage.

We found our new floating habitations much ſmaller than thoſe we occupied before, ſince they conſiſted of only one apartment; but in other reſpects they are tolerably commodious. As ſoon as our baggage was put on board, we quitted that diſagreeable place *Tſak-hau*, with a hope of meeting with others more worthy of obſervation.

At half a league thence, we approached ſo near the banks, that we might have gone on ſhore by a plank. In this part a convent ſtands a conſiderable way up the ſide of a mountain; and near the convent is a handſome octagonal tower of ſeven ſtories. Deſirous of examining the details of ſuch a building, I landed, and took a walk up the mountain's ſide. One of the bonzes came out to meet me, and ſerved me as a guide.

This convent, called *Tſak-uun-hauy-faa tſi*, is inhabited by more than a hundred and fifty monks or bonzes. The preſent Emperor has honoured it ſix times with his preſence, and has preſented it with feveral infcriptions engraved upon ftones. The principal divinity of the temple is *Sam-tfi-yu-lauy fat*.

Near the temple ftands the tower, which bears the name of *Lou-ouo-pau-thap*. One of its eight fides, meafured at the bafe, is twenty-eight feet, which gives for the total amount two hundred and twenty-four feet. On going in, I perceived that the thicknefs of the wall of the lower ftory was eleven feet and a half. At about ten feet within this wall is a fecond ftructure, the wall of which is about fix French feet thick. It contains an octagonal apartment, with a vaulted roof fkilfully turned over it, in the form of a dome. It is there that the divinity *Ouang-ming-fau-tcheou* is adored. The intermediate fpace, which feparates the two walls, or the kind of gallery they leave between them, is alfo covered by a fpherical roof, except at the part where the ftaircafe paffes through it; fo that the apartment is entirely connected and united with the walls of the tower. Thus they afford each other mutual fupport.

The fecond ftory, and thofe above it, are all conftructed upon the fame principle, with no other difference but a proportional diminution in the thicknefs of the walls. The outer wall, for inftance,

inftance, of the fourth ftory, is not more than feven feet and a half thick; and that of the internal building, correfponding with it, only three feet and a half.

Coun-yam is adored on the fecond ftory, and *Tay-tfi* on the third, while the fourth is dedicated to *Tit-fong-ouong*. The two laft ftories contain no idols, in confequence of a beam of fir, near two feet in diameter, afcending from the fixth ftory to the top of the roof. This beam which refts upon a hewn ftone in the centre of the pavement of the fixth ftory, ferves to fupport a metallic ornament ending in a point above the roof, and inferted at its lower end in the top of the beam, which alfo exceeds the height of the roof.

The galleries placed without the walls of the tower, as well as the projecting roofs, are works adapted to it, and only fupported by pieces of wood; fo that when thofe galleries and penthoufes are deftroyed by time or accidents, the tower itfelf remains not the lefs entire, as is proved by that which we faw this morning, and which I have already mentioned.

The point or fpire of caft metal is exactly of the fame form as that which I defcribed on the 18th of this month.

The height of the tower to the top of the seventh story is measured by a hundred and ninety steps, one hundred and seventy, being eight inches, and the other twenty, eleven inches high, making the total elevation about one hundred and thirty-two feet, or reckoning to the top of the roof one hundred and seventy.

The bonzes assured me that this tower has been built more than seven hundred years; but it appeared to me to be in too good preservation for a building of such antiquity, unless its outside, as well as the galleries be of more modern date.

From the description of this tower it is easy to conceive that a mass of that thickness composed of very solid bricks, may stand for ages with very little repair.

The antiquity of the tower erected in the city of Utrecht in Holland, and called the *Don*, is well known. It is true that it is built of free-stone, and not of bricks; but the latter when well baked, and held together by a good cement, do not yield in solidity to other materials, as is sufficiently proved by the duration of the buildings in which they are employed. I examined the masonry both within and without with the

utmost

utmoſt care, and I confeſs that I could not diſcover the ſmalleſt mark of decay from top to bottom: every thing looked the ſame as in a building perfectly new.

I was exceedingly happy to have an opportunity of viewing one of theſe buildings with that ſcrupulous attention which I was able to pay to this.

After having drank a diſh of tea in the great hall, I took leave of the bonzes, and returned highly ſatisfied towards my floating habitation.

On coming to the water ſide, I was witneſs to a phenomenon which in the whole courſe of my life I never ſaw before. As we are only at forty *li* from the ſea, the river partakes of the ebb and flood of the ocean. As ſoon as the tide began to make, the water ruſhed ſuddenly in, and roſe with a great deal of agitation more than a foot in two minutes. Care had been taken to remove the veſſels from the ſhore before the turn of the tide, and to ſtation them in places where there is a conſiderable depth of water, at a diſtance from one another, becauſe the rapidity of the current is ſuch as to expoſe them to be

driven

driven upon the rocks, or to be ftove in cafe of their falling aboard of each other.

As we are now at the time of the neap-tides, according to the nautical mode of fpeech, the water rofe with little force; but I was affured, and there is great probability of its being true, that during the fpring tides the water rufhes in with more violent impetuofity, and rifes to a greater height, which renders the river particularly dangerous for fhipping, efpecially when the wind blows from the eaftward. The fame phenomenon takes place in the Ganges, where it is called *Bhaar*.

During our journey from *Hong-tcheou-fou* hither we have paffed by at leaft a dozen convents, an inconteftible proof that in this part of the country the monks muft lead a moft comfortable life.

26th. As our ftay in the vicinity of *Tfak-hau* is prolonged, the Ambaffador and the reft of his fuite are gone to take a walk to the convent which I faw yefterday, and to examine it, as well as the neighbouring mountains. Having already enjoyed the charming profpect, I ftayed at home in order to commit to paper the obfervations I had yefterday occafion to make.

Experience

Experience proves to me that our prefent veffels, although not altogether incommodious, are the worft we have hitherto occupied. The failors in going from one end to the other are obliged to pafs through my apartment; and when their meals are preparing I am annoyed by the fmoke, and by the abominable fmell of the oil or greafe with which they drefs their victuals. I fhall accordingly feel lefs regret at quitting my prefent floating lodgings, than when I left the laft. Fortunately the weather continues to be very fair, which renders our voyage far lefs difagreeable than it would otherwife be.

27th. Although this day was fixed for our departure, the Mandarin of the place was fo tardy in delivering our provifions that it was two o'clock in the afternoon before we were able to fet fail. After being half an hour under way, we were obliged to take in our fails, becaufe an elbow made by the river rendered our courfe abfolutely contrary to the direction of the wind. We were therefore compelled to recur fpeedily to the tracking-line, which our prefent trackers do not handle with fo much fkill as thofe who preceded them.

Each tracker has his own line, which is very thin, but made of fome ftrong material, while all the

the veffels of the other provinces have a fingle large rope fixed to the maft, to which each tracker faftens his own little cord. This gives me occafion to reflect upon the little analogy that exifts between the cuftoms of the inhabitants of different provinces, fo that one can hardly fuppofe them to belong to the fame nation. There is fcarcely a fingle point in which they can be faid to agree. Language, drefs, covering of the head, veffels, form of adminiftration, agriculture, every thing, in a word, differs in each province. The language of the Mandarins is the only thing that is alike throughout the Empire; but from one province to another there is fuch a change of dialect, that our Canton fervants found it very difficult to underftand the language of the other parts of the country. Now if this diffonance is fo perceptible in the feven provinces we have travelled through, it is probable that it exifts in all the others. The edifices, however, as far as I was able to obferve, are all conftructed in the fame way; not only the temples and convents, but even the private houfes.

We were furrounded at fome diftance with plains immediately by the river fide, very low, and fown with turnips, and interfperfed with orchards full of peach and plumb-trees, all in flower,

with

with a mixture of bamboos. A little farther were fruit-trees in ftill greater quantity, and affording a variety very pleafing to the eye. Where the country became more mountainous, the cultivation of corn fuperfeded that of every thing elfe.

We kept along the eaftern fhore of the river, which was very wide, without appearing to have any great depth of water. At five o'clock we paffed by the village of *Ce-au-chan*, containing a number of good-looking buildings, among which are feveral diftilleries.

A quarter of an hour after we came to *Keau-fan-yen*, occupying a very large fpace along the eaft bank of the river. Here are feveral dock-yards for the conftruction of junks and other large veffels, and whole fhip-loads of oil, which gives reafon to prefume that there are oil-mills in this place. On the fide of the river, which here takes a fouth-eaft direction, the town is almoft entirely inclofed by walls of hewn ftone.

After paffing *Keau-fan-yen*, the river takes a great turn to the weft-fouth-weft, which enabled us to fet our fails again, and by their means to accelerate our progrefs. Our veffels being of

I   light

light conſtruction, ſail very faſt. We have no need to ſtop in order to eat together, as our veſſels can join each other without ceaſing to advance, the width of the river admitting of our ſailing abreaſt. At nine o'clock, however, we caſt anchor, in order that our ſailors might reſt till to-morrow morning.

At break of day the tracking-line was again brought into play, becauſe the wind which had got round to the ſouth-weſt, was conſequently become unfavourable to our progreſs.

The country, on both ſides of the river, which here grew a little narrower, was flat, and the ſoil rich and of a marly nature. The moſt elevated ſpots were covered with corn of a promiſing appearance, the others were under turnips. We afterwards ſaw a great number of fruit-trees, among which the peach was eaſily diſtinguiſhable by its bloſſoms. The mountains continued to ſhew themſelves at ſome diſtance all round us, but they were rocky and diſcovered no ſigns of vegetation, except a little bruſh-wood; and even that was hardly perceptible.

At ſix o'clock we paſſed by the village of *Fou-yang*, a well built place, and ſo agreeably ſhaded,
that

that it appeared as if it were buried among the trees. It ſtands at a little diſtance from the river.

At ſeven o'clock we were oppoſite an orchard which embelliſhed our proſpect during the half hour we were paſſing along it. Under the trees was barley already in the ear, which will no doubt be ripe before the trees, by reſuming the green garb of ſummer, can intercept the genial influence of the ſun. This fact ſerves alſo to prove that the farmers in this country know how to manage every thing with intelligence and economy.

At half paſt ſeven we had no longer plains on the north ſide of the river, which had taken a turn to the ſouth, and now ran cloſe to the foot of the mountains. We here paſſed up a narrow channel ſituated to the weſtward, and an hour afterwards found the two branches join again in one, after having formed an iſland of moderate ſize. This iſland is of conſiderable elevation, and although the ſurface is flat, and the ſoil of a fat and unctuous nature, is entirely planted with mulberry-trees, between which barley has been ſown.

At three quarters paſt eight we had the village of *Tchi-long-chan* to the north of us, a ſmall place, but containing ſome good brick houſes.

At

At the foot of the mountains is a pretty large plain, extending to the water fide, and planted as well as the other fide of the river with mulberry-trees, which makes it probable that the inhabitants employ themfelves in the manufactory of raw filk.

In one of the angles of the valley which I have juft mentioned, and upon the bank of the river, is a little fquare tower of feven ftories, built of hewn ftone.

At ten o'clock we paffed by a common hexagonal tower, alfo of feven ftories high. It is fituated upon the faliant angle of a mountain, to the north-weft, and at no great diftance from the water-fide. Its roof has fallen in, and its ornaments of caft metal are bent down on one fide. The extremity of the latter is, however, ftill higher than the top of the laft ftory.

Half an hour afterwards we doubled the flank of a mountain fkirted with fteep rocks, and arrived off the city of *Fu-yan-chen*, where we ftopped to take on board provifions.

That city, which is of moderate fize, appears to contain fome very well-built houfes. It is
fituated

fituated upon the north bank of the river, which wafhes its walls. They are built of hewn ftone, and pafs over mountains while following all the windings of the city. A part of the inhabitants are employed in the manufactory of white *Nam-kings*.

In the courfe of our navigation I obferved that a number of ftreams branch off from the river to the north-eaft. Between them are feveral flat iflands, the foil of which is of an argillaceous nature. The river itfelf molt frequently takes a fouth-weft direction, following that of two chains of high mountains which feem to approach each other in proportion as we advance.

At eleven o'clock we quitted the city of *Fu-yan-chen*, wafhed on one fide, as I have already faid, by a large weftern branch of the river, over which is a noble ftone bridge confifting of three equal arches. In the piers or uprights of this bridge are two other fmall arches, in the form of a gate, meant to give a freer paffage to the water when it rifes to that height. I gave an account of a fimilar bridge on the 21ft of February; and thefe are the only two I have met with con-ftructed in that way.

Seen at some distance in the south-west, the city makes a very splendid appearance. Behind it rise mountains of remarkable height, and the houses coated with white plaster, present a very attractive object to the eye. At the east angle, and within the walls stands a very high rock, the sides and summit of which are covered with houses and orchards, while the tower I have already mentioned, stands in a still more commanding situation. Few cities indeed can boast of a prospect surpassing that of which I am now speaking.

In the afternoon the wind favoured us by coming round to the northward. We accordingly hoisted our sails, and by its assistance made a rapid progress to the south. We had no longer any level ground to the eastward, the mountains coming close down to the water-side.

At three o'clock we found ourselves opposite the village of *Tan-tcha-coo*, a small, but very pretty place, consisting of brick-built houses, and occupying a very advantageous situation at the foot of the mountain, among an infinite number of trees of all kinds, and standing at some distance from the western bank of the river.

Soon after we quitted this village, the flat country was again succeeded by mountains, which did not begin to remove to a greater diftance, till four o'clock, when they gave place in their turn to an extenfive plain alfo on the weftern fide of the river.

At five o'clock we came to *Chan-fau long*, another village of tolerable appearance, alfo built upon the weftern bank. Behind the village is a valley of fome depth, between two mountains, entirely covered with fruit and foreft trees. Upon a fudden the river confiderably increafed its width, making, when it came near the entrance of this valley, an elbow to the weftward, which prevented its further approach.

Oppofite this village, on the eaftern fide of the river, is another, very pleafantly fituated in the midft of trees. It contains a large temple kept in very good order, and a number of good houfes built of brick. The name of this village is *Liou-cha-pou*.

Further on to the weftward, we alfo paffed a very pretty hamlet, fituated at the foot of the mountains; it is called *Sam-chan*, and is full of good houfes.

At fix o'clock we reached the village of *Ciu-tien*, ftanding in a valley in the midft of trees; and at feven we ftopped to take our ufual repaft near a guard-houfe and a triumphal arch of ftone, erected on an elevated fpot by the river-fide. Our meal being over, we continued under way till ten o'clock, when we ftopped again, in order that our people might have a good night's reft.

29th. Setting off at the dawn of day, we arrived at half paft five abreaft of the village of *Fong-cé-quan*, fituated to the eaftward. Here the river divides into two branches. We took the eaftern one, which in about a quarter of an hour brought us to the village of *Tong-tchou*, a place very thickly interfperfed with trees.

A little after fix we had to the eaftward the village of *Oung-tfan*, pleafantly feated on the fide of the river, the two branches of which meet here, and continue to flow in a fingle bed.

Before feven o'clock we had paffed by the two villages of *Tay-tchi* and *Tfy-tchi*, ftanding on the two oppofite fides of the water. The former is a large and well-built place, upon the river-fide, the bank of which is in that part of confiderable elevation. The latter, which is of lefs extent,
ftands

stands under the shade of some old trees of prodigious size.

At a quarter past seven we reached *Tay-pou*, a village situated to the eastward. The intervals left between its handsome houses are full of fruit and forest-trees, with which the whiteness of their coat of plaister forms a very charming contrast.

In this part, the river is of little depth, and its bottom is full of stones. The country on both sides changes its appearance from time to time. Sometimes it is stony and rocky, but more frequently level. In general the ground is well cultivated, part being under corn, and part laid out in orchards in which fruit and other trees are intermixed. From this slight sketch it will be easy to conceive how agreeable must be that delightfully varied prospect, the beauty of which is much inhanced by the mountains in the back ground.

At three quarters past seven we had to the eastward the hamlet of *Tsy-pou*, standing upon a hill by the river-side. To the westward is the village of *Tiou-li-tchen*, which is hardly to be discerned amid the surrounding trees.

At eight o'clock we paffed by a beautiful caf-cade, which after falling over rocks about eight feet high, mingles its ftream, which falls from the mountains with the water of the river. A little further on, but in the middle of the river, is a ledge of rocks rifing three feet above its furface.

A quarter of an hour afterwards we were abreaft of the village of *Pay-pou*, fituated on a rifing ground upon the eaftern bank, with a large pagoda of handfome appearance ftanding near it. At half paft eight we had too great brick-kilns to the eaft; and to the weft the little village of *Ou-nie-khan*, which although fmall, looks well on the outfide. Soon after we reached another village larger than the laft, called *Tcheou-tou-fong*. There, in one of the meadows that fkirt both fides of the river, was a great number of horned cattle.

At the fame place the river divides in two branches. We took the weftern one, and fteered to the fouth-weft.

At half paft nine we paffed by a pagoda called *Kiou-te-fong*, fituated at the angle of a mountain which ftands by the river-fide. The outfide is in good prefervation; the road leading up to it is
                                                                prettily

prettily planted with trees, and the pagoda itſelf is ſurrounded with pines. Between this mountain and one that follows it is a little valley entirely full of orchards and places planted with ſo much ſymmetry, that they afford a view as pleaſing as that of a garden.

A little before ten we came to the city of *Tong-lu-chen*, ſtanding by the water-ſide in a large plain terminated by two mountains. It is a pretty large place, well built with brick houſes, coaled over with plaſter, and makes altogether a very lively and handſome appearance. At its north-eaſt angle is a rock of rather remarkable form, the ſummit of which is covered with cedars and other ever-green trees. In the midſt of them ſtands a pagoda, called *Tong-ching-chun*, and a convent occupied by prieſts or monks who marry, but do not ſhave their beards. The Chineſe call them *Thaucie*. The temple, which is dedicated to *Thou-ti*, has a ſlender hexagonal tower of ſix ſtories ſtanding cloſe by it. From top to bottom it bears the marks of lightening, by which it appears to have been very much damaged. The two mountains attract the eye of the traveller to the ſame ſide, while the beautiful effect of the trees ſtanding before the city in great number

upon

upon the eaftern bank of the river is not lefs worthy of his attention.

As foon as we had advanced a little diftance beyond that city, our conductor ftood over to the weftern bank, where we ftopped abreaft of a place prepared to receive him. Our veffels followed him, and we remained there till a quarter paft three in the afternoon. In the mean time refrefhments and provifions were put on board. Then fetting off again, we had a quarter of an hour afterwards, to the eaftward of us, a hamlet called *Ou-ouaa*, fmall, it is true, but exhibiting fome handfome houfes ftanding among trees, remarkable for the beauty of their foliage and the lively colours of their bloffoms. Fields of growing corn furround this place.

During the whole day the eaftern fide kept our attention alive by conftantly reproducing all the beauties of the moft charming landfcape. The inhabitants of thefe places muft live in the enjoyment of eafy circumftances, fince we fcarcely fee a fingle habitation ill fuited to a view embellifhed by profperity.

At half paft four we had a hamlet called *Nayen-thou* to the eaft of us, with a guard-houfe ftanding standing near it. This hamlet is built along the banks of the river, and consists of neat houses, with thick plantations of trees behind them.

The river, by its shallowness, had already diminished our speed, but at half past five it suddenly contracted to one half of its width, without gaining any increase of depth. It was then that I began to perceive evident marks of a current, the river having before appeared almost stagnant, probably because we are at present in the driest season of the year, and because its wide bed is only covered by a thin sheet of water.

Stopping at six o'clock to take our usual repast, we set off as soon as it was over, and after having navigated till nine we anchored for the night, in order to give our sailors time to recover from their fatigue. The evening and the beginning of the night were rainy.

30th. The break of day was the signal for our departure. We proceeded as far as a place where the river becomes as it were a pass between two chains of high mountains. Although it had even acquired a tolerable width, it afforded no navigable channel except in the middle, that is to say, that there scarcely remained

mained a foot of water under our veſſels. In the reſt of its bed there was not ſo much as twelve inches over a bottom of large ſtones. We advanced very ſlowly becauſe our veſſels frequently got aground.

At ſun-riſe we came to a place where we were in a manner ſhut in between mountains, which, although of a rocky nature, are nevertheleſs covered with grafs and bruſh wood. They are alſo thinly interſperſed with trees, ſome of which grow even upon their ſummits, though the greater part are upon their lower extremity. But the intervals and little vallies between the mountains are filled with a profuſion of trees which form woods and groves of very pleaſant appearance.

At half paſt ſix we came to the firſt deflection in this paſs. It is at a place where there is a great opening or iſſue from between the mountains extending to the eaſtward. In this interval, and upon the ſide of the mountain, ſtands a hamlet called *Lou-ci*, with a guard-houſe or military poſt in its vicinity. This hamlet is well built of brick, and its houſes, ſcattered at a diſtance from each other, extend as far as the middle of the gorge.

At

At feven o'oclock we paffed by an imperial pagoda of great antiquity. It is fmall, but in front of it ftand three triumphal arches of ftone, and more than a dozen monuments, of ftone alfo, and loaded with infcriptions. Upon the fummit of the mountains, in the part exactly oppofite to this pagoda, which is called *Kiou-en-tay*, are two bare rocks, with a large interval between them. Upon the tabular furface of the top of thefe rocks ftand two pavilions, of which the very roofs are conftructed of hewn ftones, that they may the better defy the hand of time. According to every indication they have withftood it for centuries.

In proportion as we advanced towards the fouth, the verdure that we perceived upon the mountains loft its uniformity, the bright tints of a variety of flowers appearing defirous of outrivalling the green. One of the number was particularly beautiful. It was growing upon a fort of plant, which entwines upon hoops about a foot high, arranged on purpofe, and forms a fort of ball, covered over entirely with flowers as white as fnow.

At eight o'clock we were abreaft of a hamlet called *Ling-chu-y*, having a guard-houfe for its protection.

protection. *Ling-chu-y* is situated at the entrance of a deep glen, and at the point of an angle made by the river. It is overshadowed by a great number of trees, while little plots of land, sown with corn and turnips in front of it, give it a lively appearance, which is increased by peach and plumb trees, whose flowers are an elegant ornament to this rural prospect.

Opposite *Ling-chu-y* is another glen or valley, exactly similar to the former, with three or four houses standing in it in a delightful situation.

At nine o'clock we passed by a village called *Pamp-haa*, a place of pleasing appearance, and built of brick. It stands to the south-east and upon the mountains, while in a gorge which they leave between them at the foot of the village, is a stream of water and a number of trees.

At half past ten we had the village of *Tsik-keiou* to the south-east, situated also in a gorge upon the declivity of the mountains, and overhung by very lofty trees. At eleven we were off *Passa-sie*, much resembling *Tsik-kiou*, and standing in a similar situation.

At

At this period of our voyage we again met with fishermen training up birds to fish for them, in the way I have described on the 26th of November.

At noon we at length came to the end of the pass or narrow channel, which, on account of its length, is called *Sat-chap-li-long*, or the serpent of seventy *li*.

Beyond this pass the mountains on the east side retire to a distance, and are succeeded by low plains extending along the river side. When there we were occupied more than an hour and a half in struggling against the force of the stream, in a space of two or three *li*, where the river was so shallow that we several times touched the ground,

At half past one we reached a navigable part. The river was become more narrow than before, but it had also acquired a rapidity of stream, which, be it said *en passant*, rendered the work of the trackers more laborious, since they were obliged to exert themselves to prevent the current from turning the vessels out of their direction. The eastern bank of the river was broad and gravelly, and the ground beyond it rugged and uneven.

uneven. All the parts fusceptible of cultivation were sown with corn and turnips. The latter, which occupied the greater part of the land, were rendered very grateful to the eye by the brilliant yellow of the bloſſoms with which they were covered.

At three o'clock we had to the south-east of us a village called *Chau-li-pou*, situated upon a riſing ground by the river-ſide, and containing a number of well-built brick houſes. Half an hour after we came to another place, on the north-eaſt ſide of which a temporary triumphal arch was erected, and about fifty ſoldiers were drawn up under arms. The Ambaſſador was ſaluted with three guns, and military muſic played during our paſſage. A little farther on we had upon one ſide of us an hexagonal tower of the uſual form, ſituated upon the ſummit of a high mountain.

At a quarter paſt four we found ourſelves abreaſt of the city of *Yen-cheou-fou*, where we ſtopped, in order to take freſh proviſions on board. Two of the party availed themſelves of this opportunity to take a walk in the city, in regard to which I have to obſerve, that permiſſions of this kind

kind were every where granted us. The report they made of it was as follows:

The city is pretty large and well built; its streets are but indifferently paved, but contain handsome shops. It is situated in a great valley, entirely surrounded by mountains; the river, which here divides into two branches, running along its western side. Its walls in several places pass over the less lofty parts of the mountains. No place contains triumphal arches in greater number, since upwards of twenty were counted in only two streets. These indications of the abode of persons worthy of remembrance, mingles a sentiment of veneration with the sight of the place, to which they have given a just celebrity.

At a small distance from the city stands an Imperial pavilion. It is hexagonal, ancient, and of a handsome appearance, with a triple roof overshadowed by tall trees, but a want of repair begins to produce in it marks of decay.

Exactly in front of the city, upon a high hill planted with evergreen trees, such as pines, cedars, and cypresses, is a lofty hexagonal tower of seven stories, covered with plaster, and similar to another of which I have already spoken.

Near

Near to the one now in queſtion is a convent and a large temple, ſtanding alſo in the ſhade of trees. With what delight does the eye contemplate this noble proſpect! My teleſcope enabled me to diſcern at the ſide of this tower, and at the foot of the mountain, another convent, which is almoſt entirely concealed by trees.

At ſix o'clock we proceeded on our journey. We took the ſouthern branch of the river, whence we had a full view of the city, which affords a very pleaſing proſpect. At ſeven we made a halt to ſup, and after another hour's navigation ſtopped for the reſt of the night.

As ſoon as we came between the high mountains the river took a direction entirely weſtward.

31ſt. We got under way again at five o'clock in the morning. The river was nearly of the ſame width as yeſterday, and we had likewiſe high mountains on each ſide of us. There was, however, a greater diſtance between them and the river, ſince there was always low land on one of the two ſides of the latter, ſo that when the mountains approached one bank the other was conſtantly ſkirted by a plain, in which every little portion of ground ſuſceptible of
culture

culture was under corn, even to the very acclivity of the mountain, where fome part of the flope was cut into terraces one above another, which produced a very pleafing effect.

At fix o'clock we paffed the village *Tchap-piou*, a pretty large place, containing fome well-built brick houfes. It ftands fouth of the river, in a fpacious plain, over which trees of great age and fize throw a refrefhing fhade. We had this day thunder, accompanied by a little rain, but neither were of long duration.

I had occafion to obferve that in this river the water does not run with equal rapidity; in fome places the ftream is of remarkable ftrength, and in others it is fcarcely perceptible. I found it impoffible to divine the reafon of this, becaufe the width and the depth of the river remained the fame although thefe differences took place.

31ft. At half paft feven we paffed by a hamlet called *Than-na*, containing feveral brick houfes. It is fituated to the fouth, at the foot of the mountain, and full of trees. The lower part of the hills is moft frequently planted with pines and other large trees, while their fummits are frequently covered with trees of a different kind.

Timber for building and fire-wood are one of the principal productions of this province, where the trees grow with great luxuriancy, particularly in the weſtern parts.

At half paſt eight we reached *Tay-ang*, ſituated to the north-weſt of the river. ⁕ This place, which is pretty extenſive, conſiſts of brick houſes coated over with plaſter.

If we may judge by a great number of piles of wood, it would appear that the inhabitants of this town, as well as thoſe of moſt of the places by which we have paſſed for the laſt two days, carry on a trade in fire-wood and faggots, which are conveyed to other places by means of the river. The high grounds and mountains here afford an immenſe quantity. Almoſt oppoſite *Tay-ſang*, upon the other bank, a number of trees, intermixed with brick houſes, compoſe a very pretty hamlet.

After having gone a little further down the river we perceived at a ſmall diſtance below the ſummit of a very lofty mountain, a bare perpendicular rock of ſo dazzling a white that it ſeemed to be covered with plaſter, but on the ſides ſeveral blackiſh ſtripes were diſtinguiſhable, no doubt

doubt occafioned by the running down of the rain. It has all the appearance of a mafs of pure marble.

At nine o'clock the thunder returned with greater violence, and was accompanied by a great deal of rain, which obliged us to ftop till the ftorm difperfed. I obferved at this moment that the water had no perceptible motion. I purpofely threw feveral fmall pieces of light wood out of the veffel, but neither this means, nor the obfervation of other floating bodies, gave me the leaft reafon to fuppofe that there was any ftream.

The fun having refumed its fplendour, in half an hour we alfo refumed our journey, paffing to the fouth-eaft of the hamlet called *Maa-tcha-bau*, which is in the neighbourhood of a guard-houfe or military poft. Its well-built houfes ftand partly by the river-fide, while others extend as far as the bottom of a fmall fhady glen or valley.

At a quarter paft ten we came to a part of the river where three quarters of its width were filled with piles driven down to the edge, or left very little above the furface of the water, which here ran with confiderable rapidity.

At noon we were abreast of a village called *Chang-hau*, situated to the west of the river, and built entirely of brick.

A little further on the mountains to the eastward began to retire to a great distance, and were succeeded by large level spots. The river being very shallow in several places, rendered our navigation exceedingly difficult.

At half past one we found ourselves abreast of the village named *Thong-fou-tsa*, and at two o'clock abreast of *Tching-co-laa*. Both these places, situated to the eastward of the river, are pretty large and well built of brick. Facing the latter stands the village of *Ouing-hou t'haa*, upon the west side of the river. The mountains grew more remote before we came to this place, so that when we arrived there we had on both sides a great extent of plain, divided into cultivated fields and embellished with young trees, which continually afforded views as rich as it would be possible to meet with in Europe. In the afternoon we again had thunder accompanied with rain, which lasted till five o'clock.

It was not more than three when we arrived at a part of the river where it ran at the rate of

at

at least six miles an hour. So that, notwithstanding the united effect of the tracking line, of our sails, and of the poles with which our sailors pushed us on, it was with the greatest difficulty we could stem the stream. We at length succeeded in overcoming this obstacle. Such a difference in the movement of this river surprised me much, and nobody was able to clear up this mystery, which my own personal knowledge was altogether unable to develope.

At four o'clock, having got past the strength of the stream, and the wind being fair, we sailed along at a great rate.

Soon after we were abreast of a lofty and handsome tower of seven stories, situated to the eastward, upon a high hill. Not far from thence we passed by a village called *Tchau-fon-thaan*, a very extensive place, standing in the midst of trees on the eastern shore. Almost all the houses are of brick, and covered over with plaster, forming, with the mountains behind them, a very beautiful prospect.

Opposite, on the western shore, is a large rock of a round form, consisting of a single block. In front of this mass stands a pagoda, and at a little distance, diftance, but within it, a handfome village named *Kieou-tchen*, runs a good way inland. In this part the river had formed a large flat bank or ifland of pebbles, on each fide of which it was navigable.

At half paft four we paffed through a large village called *Tcha-ou-vou*, the river dividing it into two parts, which are well built and full of trees.

At five o'clock we had to the eaftward of *Hou-pou*, another handfome village, and a quarter of an hour after to the weftward of *Nipou*, ftanding upon a fmall eminence by the water-fide. *Nipou*, which is a pretty large place, has in a line with it, towards the plain, a village remarkable for its beauty, and ftill further embellifhed by very fine fields of corn. A great number of veffels lining the fhore from one end of *Nipou* to the other, announce it to be a commercial place.

At about two hundred toifes fouth of *Nipou*, upon the fide of a hill, ftands a pretty village called *Tfay-pou*, and in the intermediate fpace is a handfome country-houfe feated upon the bank of the river. On the eaft fhore of the latter is
alfo

alſo ſeen the extenſive village of *Tong-pou*, ſtanding in the midſt of trees.

At ſun-ſet we paſſed by a magnificent villa, ſituated to the eaſtward, belonging to a very rich man. It is compoſed of ſeveral handſome buildings covered with plaſter, the whiteneſs of which is in a manner increaſed by a black border. One of theſe buildings is three ſtories high, and in each of the two upper ſtories are four windows looking towards the river, a thing ſeldom ſeen in China, where the outſide of the houſes conſiſts only of dead walls, and where the apartments receive their light from the interior by means of court-yards. The vicinity of this habitation to the water, the moderate elevation of its ſite, the ſhade of the trees that ſurround it—every thing, in ſhort, concurs to make it a delightful abode.

At ſeven o'clock we came to a village called *Tchie-pou*, a pretty large place on the weſtern ſide of the river. Half an hour after we reached the city of *Long-ki-chen*, where we ſtopped to take our repaſt, while proviſions were putting on board for the next day. This city, which is of conſiderable extent, enjoys the reputation of producing the beſt hams in the whole Chineſe Empire.

Empire. I bought feveral of them, of which the outfide at leaft does not detract from their character.

In the courfe of the day I perceived feveral head of oxen feeding in different places, whence it appears that the inhabitants of thefe parts are not entirely deftitute of cattle.

We paffed the night at *Lon-ki-chen*.

April 1ft. At day-break we quitted the city, which at fome diftance makes by no means a defpicable appearance. It is fituated at the foot of a mountain, upon the fide of which alfo feveral of the houfes are built, and occupies an angle that the river makes with a branch falling into it from the fouth-eaft. At the fouth end of the city is an old and lofty tower, ftanding upon a hill, and ftill exhibiting in its feven ftories marks of its former beauty, although at prefent it can be confidered as little better than a heap of ruins. The rain which began at night did not ceafe with the appearance of day.

At half a league to the weftward of *Lan-ki-chen* is an infulated mountain of a long and narrow form, with a river running at the foot of it;

it; all the circumjacent country is flat and under corn. The mountainous parts are at a greater diftance. At the weftern end of this infulated mountain ftands the village of *You-ouing-chan*, a handfome and extenfive place, containing none but brick houfes, which furpafs in beauty thofe of the city. We have juft left a city that would make an equally bad figure if compared to the common run of the villages we met with yefterday.

At half paft fix we had a village called *Tcheou-ping-pou* to the eaft of us, and on the oppofite fide *Tchau-ming-chau*, the outfide of both befpeaking a fort of opulence. Shortly after we faw alfo to the weftward, but at fome diftance from the river, a pretty village called *Tfy-ming-chan*, furrounded by arable land and interfperfed with trees.

At a quarter paft feven we paffed by a place named *Nam-tcheou-ping-pou*, fituated to the eaftward on an eminence by the water fide. Several of its houfes, which are large and even two ftories high, give it a very handfome appearance.

In the province of *Tché-kiang*, where we now are, all the arable land is regularly fown in
fquares,

squares, like a draught-board, several grains of corn being put into each hole. This arrangement renders the aspect of the fields very pleasing, especially now that the corn is a foot high, and exhibits the most promising marks of an abundant crop.

Thus do the Chinese prove, in every part of the Empire, that they are no way inferior to the Europeans in the art of agriculture, and they have at the same time the advantage of being able to boast that they carried that art to the perfection at which it is now arrived, whole centuries ago, while it is only within these few years that any nation among us has thought of improving ancient methods, and even that with little success, because the farmers, slaves to habit and to the example of their forefathers, adhere with obstinacy to the old routine. In vain is it demonstrated to them that certain changes are advantageous, either in the practice of agriculture or in the treatment of cattle. This is a thing of which they cannot be persuaded.

This reminds me of a fact relating to myself, which I request the Reader will permit me to narrate:

Some

Some years have elapsed since at my house called *De Haav*, situated in the Province of Guelderland, in the United Provinces, the business of agriculture and rural economy was carried on by men in my service who executed my plans under my own direction. All my neighbours remarked and even confessed that my method of managing cattle was superior to theirs, since my cows were in as good condition, and gave as much milk in the winter as the summer. To these evident proofs I added another, it was, that my profits being increased, covered all the expences occasioned by the new system, and yet, notwithstanding so many arguments, and the effect generally expected from the impulse of self interest, no one could persuade himself to follow my example.

Before eight o'clock we found ourselves abreast of the village of *Kiou-ming-chan*, which stands at a small distance from the western bank of the river, and which appears to be a very neat town. The plains are less thickly planted with trees than yesterday.

At nine o'clock we passed by the village of *Tcheou-seo-ou*, situated like the former with respect to the river, and making a good appearance.

ance. At a quarter paſt nine we had a village called *Fi-tcho-o-oung* to the eaſtward, and *Tau-tchi-hong* on the oppoſite ſide. Both of them pretty large and well-built places.

A quarter of an hour after the long village of *Ou-tcha-u* was to the weſt of us. It is divided into ſeveral portions along-ſide of the river, and contains none but good brick houſes.

At ten o'clock we had to the eaſt of us, and at a little diſtance from the bank, *Lau-pon*, a large and handſome place, the beauty of which is much increaſed by a great number of trees. There is a military poſt cloſe to the water-ſide.

Shortly after, the river dividing into two branches forms an iſland of conſiderable elevation, which is cultivated in ſeveral parts, and at the end of which we did not find ourſelves till after a full half hour's navigation.

The bottom of the river continued to be full of pebbles, which for the moſt part are very abundant on its banks.

At eleven o'clock we came to the village of *Yu-chan-tchin*, ſtanding in a plain to the weſt-ward,

ward, and at some distance from the river, which here served to turn several mills for husking rice.

The working of these machines, consisting of a spout which is favoured by a dam, which, by raising the level of the river, increases the fall of the water, as is done in the province of *Kiang-si* in regard to the mills of which I spoke under the date of the 4th of December, and which gave me an opportunity of saying what I repeat here, that the simple construction of these machines does honour to the genius of the Chinese.

At half past eleven we passed by a village called *Than-caan*, and at noon by *Nam-than-caan*, both on the western bank. Near the latter is a guard-house, at a place where a stream coming from the westward falls into the river.

At half past twelve we came to a village called *You-cong-chan*, at which was a guard-house or military post. This village, situated upon the eastern bank of the river, is pretty large, but not so much so as the preceding ones which I have just mentioned.

At two o'clock we had *Fou-te-na* likewise to the east of us. This place, which is of considerable confiderable fize, contains fome handfome brick houfes, feveral of them being two ftories high.

By the river fide we remarked ten water mills for hufking rice. It is probable that this grain is brought here from other places; for the land lies too high to admit of much being cultivated in thefe parts. Several of the mills are now going, which confirms me in the idea I had conceived of the ufe of thefe machines.

At four o'clock we found ourfelves abreaft of *Ou-tchin*, a pretty large place, fituated upon the eaftern bank. A branch of the river coming from the fouth-eaft here falls into the principal bed; but as that branch is obftructed by a bar, it does not appear to be navigable. *Ou-tchin* contains a little hexagonal tower of fix ftories. It is very ancient, but has ftill fome remains of its former beauty. The fpire of caft metal, and the ornaments about it, of which I have already fpoken feveral times, embellifh its fummit. Nothing elfe is worthy of notice in this place, which when feen however from a little diftance, affords a very agreeable view.

Our

Our courfe, which, during the day had been generally fouth, now took a direction entirely to the weftward. At half paft four it ceafed raining, and the weather became perfectly fair.

At five o'clock we had a village called *Ou-pay-tcheou* to the north of us. It is a pretty, large place, confifting of brick houfes, and containing a number of trees which are eafily diftinguifhable, the village ftanding at no great diftance from the river. Nearly oppofite is another pretty village with lofty houfes. It is called *You-lau-chan.*

At fix o'clock we paffed by *Tchit-tou-haan,* a pretty large village to the north. Behind it and towards the plain is a flender hexagonal tower of feven ftories, ftanding on a hill. Between this village and *You-lau-chan* two tributary ftreams fall into the river, one coming from the northweft, and the other from the fouth.

A little beyond *Tchit-tou-haan* we perceived another large branch falling into that which we were in, and running in fuch a direction that the river and that branch are only feparated from each other by a narrow tongue of land partly overflown. It might even have been fuppofed

posed that the two branches made but one; but I was convinced of the contrary by obferving a little boat which was going up the other branch, and which was pushed forward by a pole applied to the tongue of land.—We stopped when we had proceeded a little farther to sup and pass the night.

During the day we faw nothing but plains and fields, growing wheat in some parts, in others rape-seed, which is beginning already to ripen.

It is eafy to conceive that we found the temperature of the air growing milder every day. Within the laft week the difference is very great. The foil appears to be here of excellent quality.

The navigation of the river was to-day much more difficult, becaufe in general it ran with greater rapidity, and becaufe in feveral places where its depth decreafed the ftrength of the ftream was ftill farther augmented. This double inconvenience materially impeded our progrefs up the river. Befides, the rain, which was accompanied by cold weather, made the labour of the trackers ftill more fevere.

We

We fet off again at break of day, ftill tracked as before, but affifted by a very fmall fail. The wind, which blew from the eaftward, allowed us to make ufe of it, becaufe we were fteering to the weftward. The weather was cloudy, and a flight mift made the air piercingly cold.

At feven o'clock we paffed along the fouth fide, which is concealed by a thick plantation of trees, and near which, at a fmall diftance from the water, ftands an hexagonal tower, of feven ftories, and of moderate fize.

To the fouth was a large hamlet, with feveral brick-kilns in the neighbourhood; while a number of water-mills for hufking rice ftood fcattered here and there upon the banks of the river.

At half paft feven we came to *Yac-tchin-fan*, a kind of advanced poft to the city of *Long-you-chen*. It is fituated at the extremity of a point of land, which divides the river into two branches, while the city itfelf is feated in the plains at five *li* diftance. *Yac-tchin-fan* is a pretty large place, and appears to carry on a confiderable trade in wood. We ftopped there to take on board provifions, and did not leave it till half paft nine.

Vol. II.   T   Almoft

Almoſt fronting it, and on the north ſide of the river, is the village of *Tſa-yu*. It is well built, and its extent beſpeaks it a place of ſome note.

A little after ten o'clock, and on the north ſide of the river, we had a ſmall chain of mountains of little elevation. The river at this part divides into two branches, which join again further to the weſtward, after having formed an iſland.

Not far from the place where it branches off we came to the village of *Tein-tia-t'haan*, where the ſtream ran ſo ſtrong againſt us, that it was with infinite difficulty we doubled a point, although our ſail was filled by a favourable wind, and we were ſtill aſſiſted by the tracking line. The rain had ſwelled the river, and increaſed the rapidity of its current.

At half paſt eleven we enjoyed the ſight of the handſome village of *Tchin-tia-th'aan*, upon the ſouth ſide. A quarter of an hour afterwards *Thing-ken-uun*, another handſome village upon the north bank attraƈted our attention.

A little

A little before I had remarked two towers at a great diftance in the plain, one to the foutheaft, the other to the fouth. I was told that the firft ftands in the city of *Long-yon-chen*, which I have juft mentioned.

The plains to the fouthward were interfperfed with a great number of trees, while thofe to the northward feem to be more particularly devoted to tillage and to fruit trees.

At half paft twelve we paffed by the village of *Long-chen-yen* aud an hour afterwards *Tang-thou-ouang*, both fituated to the northward, and making a handfome appearance.

After another half hour's navigation we found ourfelves at a village called *Yin-tchin*, which occupies both banks of the river. It was there that, for the firft time, I faw orchards of confiderable extent, entirely full of orange trees.

At two o'clock we came to *Nik-king-tchum-than*, a village of tolerable fize, and fituated to the northward, a little way behind the bank of the river, which is here very high and uneven.

A quarter of an hour afterwards a handsome village called *Tchong-ua* was to the south of us, and the great village of *Ninngau-tchan*: but the latter lies in the plain, at some distance from the river-side.

In this part the river is remarkably serpentine, and divides into several branches, which form two little islands, or rather two banks of pebbles. The stream was here also very strong.

At three o'clock we had again two pretty villages upon the opposite sides of the river; viz. *Tsiang-si* to the southward, and *Nan-ka* to the northward. To the south the plain was interspersed with small hills and rising grounds, while mountains were seen at a still greater distance.

At half past three we passed *An-cin-tchy*, standing to the southward, and surrounded by a great number of trees. Half an hour after we had to the north of us *Yan-ching-ouang*, another village, divided into four parts, and containing a number of handsome brick houses. Here the little hills on the south side began to decrease in number, and left a greater extent of level ground. The navigation of the river was still rendered laborious

and

and inconvenient by the combined effect of shoals and a rapid stream.

At a quarter past five we came to the village of *Chan-tong-chan*, pleasantly situated under the shade of trees, at a small distance from the north bank.

A quarter of an hour after we reached a village called *Ny-tchan-tau*, situated upon the side and summit of a rocky hill, and also at some distance from the water-side. Between these two places, on the banks of the river, is a vast meadow, the first of the kind that I have met with during my journey. Shortly after we came to an hexagonal tower of nine stories, in good preservation, and ornamented at the top by a handsome spire of cast metal. It stands on the north side, near the bank, is built upon a high rocky hill, and is called *Mang-tchan-thap*. It appears to have become the haunt of an immense number of herons, which are seen perched upon different parts of it, and passing to and fro between it and the river. Part of the village of *Ny-tchan-tau* is at the foot of this kind of rock, to the westward of the tower, and adds to the view afforded by the latter that of its handsome houses standing pleasantly in the midst of trees.

A con-

A confiderable number of cows were grazing in the neighbourhood, and gave new life to the picture, with which was united the profpect of another large portion of the village, ftanding further to the weftward, and inferior in no refpect to the firft-mentioned part.

At a quarter paft fix another place of the fame kind, divided into feveral quarters, and intermixed with trees, attracted my attention. It was *Saug-chuon-fuang*, which, feen from the river at this diftance, feems to have its large and handfome houfes difperfed on purpofe to render them more remarkable.

A quarter of an hour afterwards we made a ftop at a place upon the north bank, where the inhabitants fhip a great deal of charcoal made from pines burnt in the environs. Great numbers of thofe trees occupy the neighbouring heights and mountains. For the difpatch of all thefe cargoes there is only a fingle office or factory, which is built on the banks of the river, and at which the merchants engaged in this traffic affemble.

After having made a repaft oppofite this place, we proceeded upon our voyage. Shortly after we we paffed by a tower fimilar to that which I have juft mentioned : it is named *Tchien-ning-thap.* At midnight we were ftill under way. In the courfe of this day we faw a great number of mills for cleaning rice upon the two banks of the river.

3d. Scarcely had a new day appeared, when we arrived abreaft of *Kiou-tcheou-fou,* where we ftopped two hours to take on board provifions. Then ranging along it, we directed our courfe to its weftern extremity, where we made another ftop of half an hour. The city ftands upon the fouth bank; the river, which divides into two branches, forming a narrow ifland in the front of it, as long as the place itfelf. The bank upon which the walls are built is about twenty-five feet high; and two handfome gates face the river. Thefe were all I was able to diftinguifh of the city, becaufe the furrounding ramparts hid every thing elfe from our view. It appeared, however, that it was a place of moderate fize.

At a quarter paft fix we paffed between two villages, the one to the fouth called *Yat-fau,* the other to the north, both of them making a very pleafing appearance. Half an hour afterwards we had the fmall but handfome village of *Hong-tchap-pa tchap-pa* on the north bank; and at the fame time to the fouth, but at fome [diftance from the river, *Ouong-tchun-thaan*, a pretty large place. Handfome and lofty houfes, and a great number of trees, render its fituation very agreeable to the eye.

A little way beyond, the country on the fouth fide prefented broken hills to our view, that in the north had exhibited fimilar ones in the morning; and from thefe latter fome labourers were employed in extracting ftone.

At a quarter paft feven we had a beautiful profpect of a valley fituated to the fouthward, and furrounded by hills thickly interfperfed with rocks, in fpite of which the induftrious Chinefe has found means to cover all the prolific fpots with corn of the beft fort, and the moft ufeful feeds, up to the very top of the hills, by forming a kind of terrace, fuch as I have heretofore defcribed.

This valley contains within itfelf every thing that could be expected from a vaft extent of country. Not a fingle fpot of its furface is neglected. With the lively hue of various kinds of corn are intermingled the deeper tints of the orange

orange and other fruit-trees, whofe luxuriant growth, in fome meafure, rivals that of the noble pines and lofty cedars that grow upon the neighbouring heights. That nothing, in fhort, may be wanting to this charming picture, a loud-murmuring cafcade comes pouring down from the top of a rock, and runs into the middle of the valley, while the eye, which is alternately attracted by the bare parts of the rock, by the verdure of the plains, between which thofe rugged points feem to wifh to hide themfelves, and the new contraft afforded by the white foam of the falling water, is never tired of admiring a fcene fo truly picturefque, that no other part of the world is capable, in my opinion, of effacing its remembrance. So many united beauties are, however, the mere work of nature, without any other ornaments than thofe which fhe has herfelf created, or which have fprung up under the hand of the hufbandman, as fimple as herfelf. How great is the magnificence of this fituation! Yes, I will venture to fay that the moft able mafter could not reprefent the attractive view afforded by this confined fpot without weakening its effect, without fuffering a part of the charms that pervade it to efcape his pencil.

At

At three quarters paſt ſeven we arrived abreaſt of *Tſau-tſi-pou*, a pretty large and handſome place, ſituated between lofty trees, at a ſmall diſtance from the river.

A quarter of an hour after we had to the ſouth a village called *Man-tchin-ching*, a place of decent appearance, built along the water-ſide. Here the ſtony hills on the ſouth ſide retire from the river, and are ſucceeded by ſpots of level ground. Not one of theſe heights is left uncultivated. Every hill exhibits, to its very ſummit, proofs of the induſtry of the intelligent huſbandman; and as the corn is already very forward, and the turnips, which are in bloſſom, are nearly full grown, all this country forms a picture which it is more eaſy to conceive than to deſcribe, eſpecially when I add that in ſeveral places the meadows are enlivened by the peaceful animals to which they afford an abundant nouriſhment.

We are then well convinced, from our own experience, that the Mandarins did not deceive us when they aſſured us at *Pe-king* that, by taking this route, we ſhould ſee the fineſt and richeſt part of the Empire of China. And when the poor and wretched ſtate of the weſtern parts that
we

we croffed in going to the capital is confidered, and compared with the fertility and plenty which is every where perceptible in the eaft, it is impoffible to reflect, without great aftonifhment, that the Emperors have left their ancient refidence in the rich and plentiful country of *Nam-king* in order to fix it in the fandy and fterile diftrict of *Pe-king*.

At half paft eight we paffed by a village called *Nam-tchang*, fituated in the plain to the fouth, and pleafantly fhaded by trees in the midft of fields laid out with corn. A quarter of an hour afterwards we had to the fouthward the handfome village of *Tfau-tfi*, and to the north *Ouan-pou*, a tolerably extenfive and good-looking place. There are two fhoals in the middle of the river. Another hour brought us to a pretty large village called *Nau-tchun*, ftanding upon the north fide, while to the fouth, at fome diftance from the water-fide, was *Ting-tchu*, a place more confiderable than the village.

At half paft ten *Tckie-tchen*, another very extenfive village, divided into four quarters, all of which made a good appearance, appeared in the plain to the northward.

Since

Since this morning the mills for hufking rice have increafed in number on both fides of the river, and many of them are at work. The greater frequency of thefe mills having led me to make more particular enquiries, I found that I had erroneoufly conceived an opinion that the rice which is here hufked would not grow in any great quantity, on account of the elevation of the ground in thefe parts; for I learnt, with great aftonifhment, that all the fields that I now fee growing corn have produced rice, and that as foon as the prefent crops are cut down and carried, rice will in its turn fucceed them, there being two harvefts of that grain in the courfe of the year. This I have no difficulty in believing, when I fee the height of the other corn, which promifes to be fit for the fickle in four or five weeks. The rains too, which happen towards this feafon of the year, by moiftening the land, favour the germination of the rice. Befides, in cafe of neceffity, the mills are fet to work, and the water of the river fupplies the want of that which the heavens withhold. It is not then aftonifhing that all this country is in fo flourifhing a condition, fince it enjoys this double produce; indeed in every part it bears the marks of a truly delightful abode.

I col-

I collected alfo the following information concerning thefe mills: each mill belongs in common to feveral families, who have paid the firſt coſt of its conſtruction, and who defray the expences of keeping it in repair; but with this very remarkable fingularity, that all the parties concerned contribute in proportion to their fortune, although all have an equal right to the mill. One mill keeps in play fix or feven peſtles, working in as many mortars, which furniſh each fixty and fome odd pounds of huſked rice a day. It is poſſible there may be as many families intereſted in the mill as there are mortars employed.

In South Carolina in the United States of America, and at Java in the Eaſt Indies, wooden peſtles and mortars are generally ufed, but here they are both of ſtone, which certainly abridges the work. At Canton ſtone mortars and wooden peſtles are employed, becaufe the operation being performed by manual labour, a ſtone peſtle would be too heavy.

The Reader may perhaps imagine that the rice is broken by two ſtone inſtruments; but this is what I have never feen refult from the method ufed by the Chinefe. On the contrary, they abfolutely

folutely infift that the rice ferved up at table fhould combine the whitenefs of fnow with the entire prefervation of the grain.

I have, however, a remark to make upon the Chinefe mills ; it is, that their peftles work too flowly. In Carolina, in working their mills, they fo manage that each peftle ftrikes fixteen ftrokes in a minute, in order, as they fay there, to keep the rice hot, and in conftant motion.

In 1786, when I was a planter in that ftate, I had conftructed a machine according to my own ideas. Two horfes fet it in motion, and each of its peftles ftruck four and twenty ftrokes in a minute; on which account it was confidered as a great improvement. The Chinefe mills, as far as my obfervation went, give but eight or ten ftrokes in a minute. It muft at the fame time be acknowledged, that in Carolina the peftles are commonly raifed eighteen or twenty inches, while in China they are lifted from thirty-three to thirty-fix inches; which very much increafes the action of the peftle by the increafed velocity of the fall; but on the other hand, the rice remains longer without motion, which would elfewhere be confidered as a great objection. Be this as it may, it is to be prefumed, that the
                                                    Chinefe

Chinese find their method answer; or otherwise they would certainly exert their ingenuity to accelerate the movement of the wheel, and consequently that of the pestles.

With such convincing and repeated proofs before my eyes of the degree of perfection to which the Chinese have carried the art of agriculture; and recollecting again what M. Grammont, the Missionary, told me at Canton, in 1790, which I have mentioned elsewhere; that is, that at periods very remote, the Chinese have published learned books concerning this first of all arts; books, of which the translation would enrich Europe, by the depth of their theory, and by examples deduced from successful practice; recollecting these things, I say, I felt the strongest desire to obtain possession of some of their works on husbandry.

Accordingly, having an opportunity yesterday of conversing with our third conductor, a man of experience, and a well-informed literary character; he answered that each province, and even each city, has particular works upon agriculture, with precepts concerning every thing necessary to be observed by the husbandman throughout the extent of their district; that these books are kept

kept as facred things, and depofited in the hands of commandants or governors of cities, who are not permitted to entruft them to any one; and that confequently it is in vain to think of procuring them, becaufe they are not to be fold. The Mandarins of the cities are bound to give to the individuals within their diftrict all the information that the latter may afk for, which feldom happens, becaufe a knowledge of agriculture, held in efteem for feveral centuries paft, has been tranfmitted from generation to generation; from father to fon, with every particular of both theory and practice. This has rendered the fcience fo general, that it is fcarcely poffible for any one to ftand in need of further inftruction. He promifed me, however, to ufe his beft endeavours to procure me the works which treat of cultivation in the province of Canton.

At three quarters paft ten, we paffed along *Tchie-than*, a very neat village, fituated upon the fouthern bank. Here is a great fhoal in the midft of the river.

At noon we came to *Pau-yuu*, a place ftanding to the fouth, occupying a great extent along that bank, and containing a great number of large and lofty houfes, with windows in both
ftories

stories looking towards the river. Upon an eminence oppofite ftands *Cau-tchie.*

At one o'clock we came to another village, called *Kiou-tau-than.* It is a place of fome extent, fituated behind the lofty fouthern bank, and entirely furrounded by trees.

To the north, the hills or little mountains have again advanced as far as the river fide. The great mountains which terminate the horizon on both fides are alfo lefs remote, fo that the quantity of level ground is diminifhed, and we even perceive by the diftance that it will grow fmaller ftill.

All the country we faw this morning was beautiful, and embellifhed by an abundance of foreft trees, and a great number of orange-groves, which produce a very agreeable variety.

At two o'clock we came to *Tchau-yu,* a village ftanding in an elevated fituation, although by the river-fide. It is built at the foot of a little mountain, and entirely covered with pines. Near this village, which is of meaner appearance than thofe which precede it, is a guard-houfe, or military poft.

VOL. II.   U   Half

Half an hour afterwards, the north fide of the river prefented to our view a large piece of meadow ground, in which a confiderable number of cattle were grazing. In general we have feen more to-day than for feveral days paft.

At three o'clock we were oppofite a beautiful cafcade, which falls with impetuofity down the mountain fide, and which after dividing into three branches, rufhes furioufly over the rocks, which feem to oppofe its inclination to mingle its waters with that of the river.

The latter, a little before it reaches this place, receives a branch coming from the fouth-eaft, which only leads to a new feparation half an hour afterwards, and to the formation of an ifland of fome height, and in a good ftate of cultivation.

At three quarters paft three the foot of the high mountains on the fouth fide advanced as far as the bank, while on the north fide there was ftill an intermediate fpace of level ground. Here a ftorm arofe, which terrified our Chinefe failors to fuch a degree, that they carried us clofe into the fhore, in order that we might take fhelter under it. A heavy fhower of rain coming on afterwards,

wards, we refolved to ftop at this place for the whole of the night.

The weather was fo hot to-day, that Fahrenheit's thermometer rofe to 79 degrees.

Being very near the place whence we are to make a journey of about a hundred *li* over land with all our baggage, the rain is a matter of fome concern to us, as we are apprehenfive of its rendering the roads execrably bad.

4th. A frefh and fair breeze induced us to fet off at half paft five; for otherwife the rain and a ftrong current would have kept us where we were.

Our veffels being light, and drawing little water, go very faft, and in my opinion at not lefs than the rate of ten thoufand toifes an hour; but fuch is the rapidity of the ftream, that if our way be meafured by the time we employ in going from one point to another, we do not advance at above a third of that rate.

At half paft fix we were a-breaft of a village called *Chang-ou*. It ftands at no great diftance from the water fide, towards the fouth-eaft, at the foot of mountains, which afterwards turn off to the fouth.

At this place, the river by dividing into different branches, forms feveral iflands and a number of fand-banks. It was very much fwelled by the rain-water, which came pouring down from the mountains on every fide, forming cafcades in its way over the rocks.

At a quarter paft feven we paffed *Maa-tfu,* a very large village fituated to the fouth-eaft, and compofed of three detached portions, receding one behind another from the water fide into the plain. The houfes for the moft part are handfome. That part that runs along the river fide contains a ftone bridge of a fingle arch, built over a confiderable ftream, which mixes its waters with thofe of the river. The bridge is in very good condition. Towards the middle of it, but upon one of its fides, is a ftone pillar, with a lantern upon the top of it, in which is placed a lamp, that ferves, during the night, as a guide to paffengers.

While paffing by feveral water-mills, I obferved that the great wheel, by means of a little wheel, which revolves at the other extremity of

the

the fame axle, and which ferves to turn a horizontal wheel, gives motion to mill-ftones, that ftrip the rice of the outer hufk before it is carried to the mortar, in order to be cleanfed from its inner one. This fingle machine then ferves at one and the fame time, to remove the outer hufk, and to cleanfe the rice, a double effect which I never faw produced by any machine in Carolina, where the firft operation is feparately performed in wooden mills.

At three quarters paft feven we paffed by *Suy-laam*, fituated to the fouthward.

The wind frefhening, we were obliged to reef our fails, which was not done till a veffel, having the fervants of one of the Mandarins on board, had the misfortune to overfet. At a fmall diftance from thence, we were almoft entirely furrounded by mountains, having only a little level ground to the north. Thefe mountains are almoft bare, are deftitute of trees, and afford nothing but a few worthlefs herbs, moffes, and other plants which generally grow upon rocks.

At half paft nine, being near *Sam-ti-than*, a hamlet ftanding at an angle made by the river, we entered into another branch of it, which takes a south-west direction, while the main stream runs to the north-west. We were now at no great distance from the city of *Chang-chan-chen,* where we are to quit our present vessels. In a number of reaches the wind was unfavourable, and the stream very strong, which gave a great deal of trouble to the crew, and was the occasion of our not arriving before eleven o'clock at the place where vessels usually stop a-breast of *Chang-chan-chen*. At his arrival the Ambassador was saluted with three guns, and the same honour was afterwards paid to me.

The city of *Chang-chan-chen* is very ancient, but not large, although its walls are very extensive, and pass over two mountains. Within them are to be seen the ruins of a very ancient tower, which stands upon a high hill, and of which six stories are still discernible. There is nothing else curious, nor any kind of manufacture or particular trade worthy of observation in this place. Its whole importance is derived from its serving as an *entrepôt* for all the merchandize that the provinces of *Tché-kiang* and of *Kiang-si* send reciprocally to each other.

We had been half an hour at *Chang-chan-chen*, when our third conductor came to pay us a visit, and

and delivered to me an itinerary of the route we are to take to-morrow if the weather permit. It includes a space of ninety *li* (eight leagues and a half). He begged us in consequence to breakfast early in the morning, in order that we may take our evening repast on board of the vessels in which we are to embark. On this account our cooks will be sent off at an early hour.

I immediately repaired to the Ambassador, to acquaint him with this plan. He agreed to it, provided it should not rain, not wishing to expose our baggage to injury, nor to suffer any inconvenience himself, since nothing required our reaching our journey's end on any particular day. Our arrangement is therefore entirely conditional.

The weather was to-day rendered cold by the rain; and the wind freshened in the afternoon.

We learned with great satisfaction that nobody was lost by the oversetting of the *Sampane*, which carried the soldiers of a provincial Mandarin, by whom we are escorted. We should have felt doubly hurt, if this mark of honour shewn to the Embassy had occasioned the lofs of a single individual.

END OF VOL II.

Notice of a Collection of Chinese Drawings, in the Possession of M. Van Braam, Author of this Work.

I.

GEOGRAPHY.

A volume of coloured maps, of about fifteen inches long by a foot high; exhibiting all China, divided into provinces.

II.

VIEWS AND LANDSCAPES.

Seven volumes containing three hundred and sixty-eight drawings; being so many coloured views and landscapes representing the most interesting places in all China.

Each drawing is eighteen inches long by thirteen and a half broad.

This part, which is the most extensive of the collection, and that which also required the most time to collect, was formed by the opportunities which a variety of of circumstances gave M. Van Braam of obtaining copies of pictures; 2dly, and more particularly by the idea which he conceived of sending Chinese painters to travel at his expence throughout the whole of China; in order that they might collect views of every thing curious and picturesque which that country contains. 3dly, by the opportunity the Dutch Embassy gave him of seeing a number of remarkable things, and sketching them himself, that he might have them afterwards painted at Canton, as he says himself in several parts of his narrative.

That journey, before which M. Van Braam was already in possession of drawings of a great number of the places which lay upon his road, either in going to *Peking*, or on his return from thence, served to convince him of the fidelity of the painters who had enriched his collection with them; and naturally induced a belief that an equal attention had been paid to truth, with regard to places which he had no opportunity of seeing.

So great a number of drawings afford a great variety, and are highly gratifying to curiosity.

In the first place they give an exact idea of the general appearance of China; of its plains; of its mountains, which have a character that seems to be peculiar to them; and of its rocks, the form of which is in general strange and whimsical, when compared with those of Europe. They are often composed of blocks of greater or smaller magnitude, the rhomboidal regularity of which is striking. It is not uncommon to see some which are arched, and which leave between the kind of
pillars,

pillars, or masses that support them, great open spaces, the boldness of which astonishes, especially where they stand over streams of water, as if intended for bridges by the hand of nature.

A view of rivers, of immense navigable canals, of dikes, of causeways, of the means of irrigation, and carrying off the water; of cascades, &c. frequently add to the interest of the picture.

It is gratifying to have a sight of a Chinese city, of the walls that surround it, and of the different monuments it contains; as well as to judge of the style of the architecture, and of the ornaments which it borrows from the chissel of the carver, and from the art of the gilder and varnisher.

In one drawing is an extent of country, embellished by all the charms of cultivation: trees, meadows, plants, animals, husbandmen, every thing, in short, puts in its claim to attention. In another is one of the Emperor's summer-palaces: in a third, a spot embellished by the pride of a Mandarin, or by the luxury of a private individual; while in a fourth it is the care taken to provide an asylum for pleasure, a dwelling for fanatical bonzes, or a retreat for philosophy that occupies the mind.

A perspective view of a castle, or of a guard-house, near which are soldiers differently clothed and armed; and that of an esplanade with large bodies of troops exercising, ercifing, alfo prefent themfelves. High-ways, magnificent bridges, colleges, academies, bells, antique vafes, places devoted to the dead; and clocks, which announce to man, that time, while flying carries him away, fuccceffively offer themfelves to the eye of the obferver.

In looking over this collection of views, it is eafy to conceive how great is in China the activity of agriculture and commerce, thofe two great fprings of political movement. Almoft in every drawing are feen a number of veffels paffing through the Empire in every direction. The beholder is ftruck with the variety of fhipping, adapted to the different rivers and canals; and he ftops with pleafure in places intended for embarkation and debarkments, which themfelves give life to the picture. The various kinds of merchandize; the means ufed for the carriage of each of them; all that induftry has conceived and executed to overcome the obftacles that nature fometimes oppofes to it; and particularly that of the difference of levels between the water of feveral natural or artificial canals which communicate with one another, are fo many fubjects of inveftigation, amufement, and inftruction.

It is impoffible to examine this collection of drawings, without deriving from it another advantage—that of difcovering in the inhabitants of China feveral traits which prove that their ideas are not always without fome analogy to our own. This is, for inftance, obfervable in a view of a temple of the God of Riches, to which thofe are thronging, who wifh to folicit his favours.

Among

Among the public edifices are salt magazines, and innumerable towers; with convents, pagodas, and mosques, which furnish a new proof that superstition is so powerful, only because she persuades man that she protects his weakness. The construction and decorations of these buildings often possess beauties, which, though dissonant from our taste, are not the less real.

We experience a different sort of sensation when we come to twenty drawings, which are so many views of different parts of the buildings erected in the European manner, within the immense circuit of the walls of the Emperor's summer palace of *Yuen ming-yuen*. When we know that this habitation is only one out of thirty-six occupied by the Emperor and his suite in that palace, we are naturally led to form a magnificent idea of the country, in which the gigantic plan of this imperial residence has been conceived and executed.

When after this we come to a representation of some cavernous mountains, and especially when we meet with that which exhibits men in a state next to savage, and without communication with the Chinese, whose language they do not even speak, it requires an extraordinary effort of the mind, to conceive the idea of a state which combines with an almost unlimited extent, a population we are tempted to believe fabulous, and an antiquity which has no longer any contemporary.

Perhaps this interesting part of M. Van Braam's collections has not always in the accuracy of drawing, or
in

in the colouring, what European eyes are accuſtomed to deſire; but when we reflect that it is China that is meant to be repreſented, and that Chineſe are the painters, we are diſpoſed to believe that in ſome reſpects this manner is not without its advantage; and that the reſemblance gains a great deal that it might have been robbed of by the more delicate hand of an European.

III.

VIEWS AND MONUMENTS OF CANTON.

Two volumes containing a hundred and ten coloured drawings, which are ſo many views of edifices and monuments in the immenſe city of Canton.

Each drawing is eighteen inches long by thirteen inches high.

As Canton is the only city in China where foreigners are allowed to land, and as even there they are only permitted to appear a few months every year within the limits of the ſuburbs, in which they are in a manner confined, it may be ſaid with truth, that it is by Canton alone that the Europeans can judge of the whole Chineſe empire.

This is then a powerful motive of attention to a ſet of a hundred and ten drawings, which exhibit every thing remarkable in that city, independently of ſeveral other drawings compriſed in that part of M. Van Braam's collection,

collection, containing the views and landscapes of which I have already spoken.

A city of astonishing population; a city become the *entrépôt* of almost all the foreign trade carried on by the Chinese, must offer to the eye of the observer a multitude of curious things of every kind.

Among them are a great number of pagodas and convents, exhibiting along with their different details the most strange and monstrous productions of superstition; palaces in which the civil and military governors reside; monuments serving as so many asylums for the wretched of every description, age, and sex; edifices occupied by the different branches of public administration, rice and salt magazines, an arsenal, &c. &c.

These drawings afford us an opportunity of studying and comparing the civil, military, and religious habits, as well as the manners and usages of the country. From them we may derive a knowledge of several arts, of the processes they employ, and of the manner in which the Chinese apply them in their different kinds of architecture, and in decorating, ornamenting, and furnishing all kinds of edifices and monuments whatever.

These two volumes also afford a variety of means of judging of the effect produced upon the Chinese mind, by an assemblage of men which perhaps surpasses that of the largest cities in Europe; and the philosopher and the moralist may there find more than one subject for reflection on seeing that man, whatever part of the globe he he may inhabit, always unites in his conduct, his conceptions, and his works, the moſt ſtriking contradictions.

Some of theſe drawings alſo repreſent public executions. Guilt is then the produce of every ſoil; and it will doubtleſs appear that the neceſſity of puniſhing has not been combined in China with the principles which humanity dictates in favour even of the greateſt criminals.

IV.
THE PAGODA HAAY-TSONG-TSI.

In the Iſland of Honan, oppoſite Canton, with the Temples, the Convent, the Buildings belonging to it, &c.

This volume contains forty-eight drawings, eighteen inches long by thirteen high.

The artiſt has endeavoured, by the numerous details contained in them, to give an exact and complete idea of every thing belonging to a celebrated pagoda, which ſeems calculated to intereſt Europe more than any other, becauſe it was within its walls that the Engliſh Embaſſy of Lord Macartney was received at Canton and had an audience of the *Tſong-tou*, and becauſe the Dutch Embaſſy which gave occaſion to the preſent work had there alſo ſeveral audiences of that Viceroy [*].

[*] Lord Macartney's lodgings were in the garden of a merchant named *Lopqua*, ſeparated from the convent of this pagoda by nothing but a wall, in which is a door of communication that ſerved the Ambaſſador as a paſſage from one to the other.

A bird's-eye

A bird's-eye view shews the whole assemblage of edifices of which this pagoda is composed, and the rest of the drawings exhibit a variety of details, particularly very rich idols, figures, and statues, which to us are certainly entirely new.

V.

MYTHOLOGY.

Two volumes, containing each a hundred and fifty drawings of seventeen inches high by a foot in breadth.

This part of the collection exhibits the figures of a hundred gods and goddesses, and of several personages considered as the ministers, agents, or servants of an Almighty Being, of a God superior to all others.

Among these divinities, lightning, thunder, wind, rain, fountains, fire, cooks, and carpenters, have theirs. We also meet with those of goodness, prosperity, secrecy, fertility, and immortality; as also a god who protects against injustice and the violence it does not scruple to employ; and another who saves from despair. The healing art has its god, the physicians have another, and death has also his.

In this set of drawings, which represent the whims and weaknesses of the human mind, at the same time that they discover some ideas that do it honour, the observer may perceive analogies, study the immediate and remote relations of certain attributes, and convince himself of the extravagant lengths to which the ima-
X gination

gination is capable of going when it takes superstition for its guide.

These drawings are also remarkable for the richness of their colouring, and for the success of the painter in representing the dresses in which the divinities have appeared to the Chinese through the medium of those who no doubt think, that the better to command the respect of the vulgar, gold and silver, which are also divinites, ought to shine upon them intermingled with the most brilliant colours.

VI.

HISTORY.

Three volumes containing a hundred and twenty drawings.

Here we may trace the successive discovery or rather invention of the arts in China. Man, in his primitive simplicity, and half naked, exercises his industry by degrees, and becomes hunter and fisher. He constructs dwellings to shelter him from the inclemency of the seasons. From the very employment of his natural means, from his inclination to society, proceeds civilization; his strength and his intelligence increase by his union with other men; he becomes a cultivator, and after having defended his crop from the ravages of animals, he thinks of subjugating some of them in order to make them assist him in his labours. Thus do we see the birth of rude but useful arts: these indicate at a distance, more or less difficult to measure, those of a politer

politer kind. With fo many new ideas arifes the neceffity of expreffing and tranfmitting them, which at length produces the efforts and the fuccefs of genius.

By entering into thefe details, fuggefted by the drawings themfelves, it is not meant to give a complete idea of them; for the above view of things belongs to the hiftory of every people and of all nations, while that of China has its peculiar characteriftics. They are the more curious to ftudy in thefe hundred and twenty drawings, as they are in fact fo many pictures of eighteen inches by fourteen broad, in each of which a fubject is prefented embellifhed with, or at leaft accompanied by all the interefting acceffories the painter has been able to add: battles on land, fea fights, encampments, conflagrations, and various other fcenes of deftruction; every thing bears a character which affords room for more than one obfervation. The accuracy of the drawing, the frefhnefs of the colours, every thing, in fhort, combines to render the fubject more interefting; while in architecture, in ufages, in habits, in furniture, in productions of the three kingdoms, in landfcapes which exhibit a country little known, thefe two volumes furnifh details, all of which are worthy of praife.

VII.
MANNERS AND CUSTOMS.

A volume containing twenty-four drawings, each feventeen inches long by thirteen broad.

The circumftances which belong to the different ranks in China, or which ferve to characterize them, have been applied to the different periods of human life.

Here then we difcover the different gradations from the birth of a child to the death of a man, with the intermediate occurrences of education, admiffion among the men of letters, honours paid to the Mandarins, ficknefs, &c. &c.

The drawings are coloured as well as all the reft of the collection.

Two volumes containing a hundred drawings, thirteen inches high by a little more than nine inches broad.

Thefe are fo many coloured performances reprefenting the primitive inhabitants of China; the firft Emperors and their wives; Confucius; the Emperor *Kienlong*, to whom the Embaffy was fent; the Emprefs, his wife; principal Minifters of State; Mandarins of all ranks; military candidates exercifing themfelves in order to merit promotion; foldiers of all defcriptions; inhabitants of town and of country; players; beggars; male and female bonzes; the different individuals compofing the train of Mandarins, &c. &c.

The end of thefe two volumes is compofed of fifteen drawings, reprefenting different kinds of torture and punifhments in ufe in China, almoft all of which exhibit a degree of cruelty highly afflicting, both becaufe it can have been thought neceffary, and becaufe it is infufficient to prevent the commiffion of crimes.

PARTI-

PARTICULAR MANNERS OF THE CLERGY.

Two volumes containing each fifty coloured drawings, feventeen inches long by thirteen inches broad.

The firft of thefe drawings reprefents the introducduction of idolatry into China, and all the reft ferve to prove the prodigious fuccefs it has obtained. By going through this collection a complete idea is obtained of all the ufages and ceremonies of the Chinefe clergy, which is compofed of both fexes.

There, as well as elfewhere, the manners of the clergy, which, properly fpeaking, conftitute its hiftory, are diftinguifhed by traits characteriftic of the blindeft credulity, kept up and ftrengthened by hypocrify, which teaches what it does not believe; and by fuperftition, the minifters of which counfel and preach by turns whatever it has made them adopt.

True philofophy cannot help deploring both thefe errors, and the abfurdity of worfhipping idols; but will it be able to cure human reafon?

GAMES.

A volume in which are thirty-two drawings, fixteen inches long by thirteen inches broad.

They reprefent a like number of games with which the Chinefe exercife or amufe themfelves. Among them we recognize thofe of the fcourge-top, quoits, and bowls.

All thefe drawings are coloured; each contains feveral figures, and the ftudy of manners and *coftume* may alfo derive fome advantage from them.

VIII.
ARTS AND TRADES, AGRICULTURE, MANUFACTURES, FINE ARTS, &c.

Two volumes containing each fifty coloured drawings, which reprefent different Chinefe arts and trades, with figures in action, and ferving to characterize each profeffion.

This part of the collection, which is executed in a very pleafing manner, affords a knowledge of feveral tools; of a variety of utenfils, and of the form given to them; as well as feveral articles of furniture. They alfo give us an exact idea of the habits of the people; indicate their ufages; and fometimes exhibit traits of the Chinefe character.

A volume containing forty-eight drawings, fifteen inches long by a foot broad, viz.

Twelve drawings relative to the culture and preparation of rice.

Six drawings relative to the cultivation of the cottontree, and to the preparation and working up of the cotton.

Six drawings which exhibit the mulberry-tree, the breeding of filk-worms, and the preparation of the beautiful fubftance which that infect produces.

Eight

. Eight drawings which contain details of the art of making porcelain.......

Four drawings exhibiting operations belonging to a pottery.

And, laftly, twelve drawings all relative to the culture and gathering of the different forts of tea.

Each drawing is a picture in which a number of individuals of both fexes are feen in action. But what renders this part of the collection particularly interefting is its not containing a fingle drawing that is not at the fame time a delightful landfcape, in which the painter has collected, with a remarkable degree of truth, every thing that is moft agreeable and ftriking in China, either in fituations, mountains, rivers, ftreams, trees, fruit, flowers, habitations, inftruments of hufbandry, their different ufes, &c.

In the procefles of the arts the fame variety is to be found; and the fame information is to be gained from a reprefentation of a number of machines and different tools: in a word, it is impoffible to examine thefe defigns, all drawn, coloured, and fhaded with remarkable tafte, without beftowing praife upon the painter who produced them, and who found means to intermix with a number of ufeful procefles, curious details relative to the *coftume*, and even traits of character of feveral claffes of Chinefe.

X 4   A volume

A volume containing two drawings relative to the manufactory of glafs, thirteen inches long, by eleven wide.

A fifherman.

Two drawings relative to printing.

Four concerning the art of making porcelain.

Thefe feven are eleven inches long, by thirteen inches high.

Eleven drawings, exhibiting games, among which is the fwing; tumblers, and performers of fleight of hand; a fortune-teller, &c.

Musick.

A volume, in which are thirty-three coloured drawings reprefenting a like number of women playing upon different mufical inftruments in ufe in China.

From this volume we get a knowledge of thofe inftruments, and a good idea of the female dreffes.

Each drawing is fixteen inches wide, by thirteen inches broad.

Ships,

SHIPS, VESSELS, BOATS, AND BARGES.

Two volumes, containing each a hundred and fifty drawings, sixteen inches and a half broad, reprefenting veffels of all kinds, fuch as are employed in China in the different branches of navigation.

They are all drawn and coloured after nature, fo that a judgment may be formed of all the modes of Chinefe naval architecture, from fhips of war down to the fmalleft boat. The external ornaments, the internal details, the contrivances ufed in the navigating of the different veffels; every thing in fhort is expreffed.

Here we diftinguifh the Emperor's *Sampane*, or pleafure barge, which is denoted by a kind of dome with peacock's feathers and five-clawed dragons upon it; other *Sampanes*, from that ufed by the Mandarin of the firft rank, or by the courtezan who abandons herfelf to the votaries of pleafure, down to that which waits in expectation of being hired by the private individual.

In this collection are alfo found veffels for long voyages, coafting barks, *junks*, yachts, *fapentines*, cuftomhoufe boats, thofe that are required by the depth of different rivers, either for travelling or for the conveyance of falt, rice, cotton, tea, faggots, oil, ftones, &c. thofe in which tradefmen of different kinds difplay and carry about the articles they wifh to difpofe of, among which we fee the fhop of the butcher, florift, fruiterer, &c.

The

The different kinds of fishermen's boats, passage vessels or hoys, and the boat that serves for breeding ducks and the hatching of their eggs make part of this collection.

In it are also to be found the rafts that carry rice, fire-wood, and timber for building; a sort of boats constructed for speed, and in general employed at certain times of the moon in matches, in which the sailors endeavour to display their talents and their strength, and to outgo one another.

Among these vessels some go with one or more sails; others with oars, and others again with paddles. Those meant for matches are of the last kind, and carry as many as six and twenty men. The rivers are sometimes navigated by means of the tracking-line, and even of poles, as is stated in the Journey of the Dutch Embassy.

Independently of the variety that the things themselves produce in these two volumes, the eye is delighted with the accuracy of the drawing, and with the elegance and the delicacy of the details. The observer also draws from them ideas concerning the habits of the Chinese, and a number of customs, particularly that of indicating, by established signs, the habitual or momentary destination of the vessel, or the quality of the persons it is conveying.

Finally, when we reflect that in China several millions of individuals are born and die on board of vessels without ever possessing any habitation but these floating
houses

houfes, in which whole families lead a fort of amphibious life, we feel a ftill ftronger intereft while examining this collection, which at the fame time calls to mind the moft daring attempt of man.

IX.
NATURAL HISTORY.
Fish, and Crustaceous Animals.

Two volumes containing eighty drawings, a foot long by about nine inches high, in which are drawn and coloured after nature frefh and falt-water fifh, feafnakes and eels, lobfters, and fhrimps, the thornback, the mackarel, the fwift-fwimming trumpet-fifh, the voracious fhark, &c. &c.

An idea may be formed from thefe two volumes of the advantage poffeffed by the Chinefe painters in the ufe of gold and filver. The laft metal efpecially, when employed in painting the fcales of a fifh, gives a fingular degree of truth to the touches of the pencil. It is no exaggeration to fay that thefe animals appear alive upon the paper, on which the artift has reprefented them with a degree of care that has preferved every trait, and all the delicacy of the model.

Birds.

A volume confifting of fifty drawings, fifteen inches and a half long by fourteen inches high.

Thefe

These drawings, full of different birds, and coloured after nature, are moſt beautiful pieces. The painter ſeems to have taken particular pleaſure in the repreſentation of thoſe charming creatures, whoſe forms, more or leſs various, more or leſs elegant, are all embelliſhed by a robe, in which nature diſplays her moſt brilliant tints, combined with a degree of taſte which belongs to her pencil alone.

While viewing this ornithological part of the collection, while admiring theſe intereſting animals which ſeem to breathe, it is impoſſible to avoid remarking the art with which the painter has placed them upon the different plants which each ſpecies affects, and in the moſt elegant attitudes. We thus enjoy a double pleaſure, while learning ſomething of their nature and habits. The aquatic bird ſometimes diſcovers traits, which are the more eaſily perceptible, becauſe he is aſſociated in the ſame drawing with a land bird; while two different plants, by being brought together, ſtrike the eye more forcibly, and make an agreeable contraſt with the water, which indicates the inclination of the animal capable of exiſting in both elements.

When the male and female of the ſame ſpecies have any remarkable difference in their forms or feathers, that difference has been obſerved and expreſſed.

It is in this part of the collection that we are never tired of admiring the art of employing thoſe beautiful colours that ſeem to belong excluſively to Aſia. It is ſo much

much the more valuable, as the plants, flowers, and fruit introduced along with the birds make it an excellent fupplement to the other volumes fet apart for the vegetable reign.

We are pleafed alfo to find in it feveral birds of other climates, which belong alfo to one of the three parts of the globe, and fometimes to them all.

INSECTS, REPTILES, AND CRUSTACEOUS ANIMALS.

A volume containing forty-fix drawings, of about a foot long by nine inches high, in which are drawn and coloured after nature, infects, reptiles, cruftaceous animals, &c. Among them we particularly remark the bee, the wafp, feveral fpecies of the dragon-fly, crickets, grafshoppers, fpiders, cock-roaches, a variety of flies, wood-lice, miliepedes, beautiful butterflies and caterpillars, fnails, the toad, the frog, the crab, the mountain crab, the mabouya, the fmall lizard, the viper, &c.

The truth with which every thing is reprefented, even in the moft minute details, the beautiful colours which embellifh thofe different animals, and which feem ftill more brilliant in the butterflies, cannot fail to charm the eye of the naturalift.

FLOWERS.

Three volumes containing a hundred and forty-eight drawings of flowers, drawn and coloured after nature.

In

In three of thefe volumes, and particularly in one of them which contains fifty-eight drawings, each flower is feen upon a bit of the plant, fhrub, or tree, to which it belongs, fo that a judgment may be formed of the colour and nature of the bark; of that of the leaves, of all the parts of efflorefcence, and fometimes even of thofe of fructification.

Among thefe flowers, of which the greater part to other parts of the world, are the everlafting, the poppy, different kinds of rofes, the narciffus, fun-flower, lilack, various fpecies of pinks, the auricula, grenadilla, balfam, tube rofe, great nightfhade, apocynum, the flower of tobacco, of the cotton-tree, of the orange, of the palmachrifti, &c.

It would be impoffible to exprefs the truth with which thefe flowers are painted. The talents of the Chinefe. in this way are well known, and a well-merited homage is paid to them on feeing what they have produced in this collection. The eye is as much delighted as it can be by an imitation which exhibits all the grace and all the delicacy of the original.

Each drawing is fifteen inches high by twelve broad.

FRUITS.

A volume in which are forty eight drawings of fourteen inches high by eleven broad, exhibiting an equal number of fruits almoft always placed upon a bit of the branch, and fometimes even upon the flowers.

The

The apple, pear, grape, peach, plumb, pomgranate, *Le-tchi*, rose, apple, (*la pomme rose*), shaddock, walnut, the averrhoa, orange, banana, &c. &c. are among the productions inserted in this volume; and the just praise given to the flowers is also due to the fruit.

PLANTS, TREES, SHRUBS.

A volume containing thirty-six drawings fifteen inches and a half long by thirteen inches high.

These are so many trees kept in a dwarf state. They resemble little old men, who should unite the characteristicks of youth and vigour with those of age. This class of vegetables in which man has strangely associated the two extremes, are much esteemed in China, and cultivated with great care in their courts and gardens.

They are painted and coloured after nature, and represented entire; so that an exact idea may be formed of their general appearance, and of their foliage. For this part of the collection such objects have been selected as the Chinese prize the most.

Truth in the imitation, brilliancy of colouring, and beauty of design, every thing in short is united; and to give these drawings an additional grace, the painter has put each tree in a vase of which the form is constantly elegant, although it varies continually as well as the colours he has chosen, either for the purpose of making
them

them harmonize, or contraſt agreeably with that of the tree itſelf; in a word, the moſt exquiſite taſte has directed the whole of this work.

Independently of theſe thirty-eight volumes, containing about eighteen hundred drawings, which I have juſt mentioned, and diſtinguiſhed by the title of M. Van Braam's Collection of Chineſe Drawings; independently of a number of maps, charts, and plans, ſome of which relate to the preſent work, and of drawings that are not contained in the thirty-eight volumes already enumerated, M. Van-Braam has brought over a very conſiderable number of other curious things, which are intended to ornament his houſe and apartments; and of which the nature and taſte are calculated to ſuit their deſtination.

Among theſe things I muſt particularly ſpecify four.

One is a vaſe of rock cryſtal, ſupported by the trunk of a tree, and embelliſhed with a garland of flowers. This vaſe, which is eight inches high, and thirteen inches in circumference at the middle, conſiſts with all its acceſſories of a ſingle ſtone. This beautiful cup, the dimenſions of which alone would make it a rarity, is alſo deſerving of admiration, on account of its external workmanſhip, which is exquiſitely finiſhed, and on account of the labour to hollow it and poliſh the inſide.

The ſecond conſiſts of two pictures three feet long by two feet high, in each of which, upon a tree of brown ſandal wood, ornamented with branches, leaves, and flowers,

flowers, of different kinds, skilfully shaded, are fifty birds, making twenty-five couple, all of ivory, and coloured after nature.

Taste has so happily presided over the composition of these pictures, that the eye discovers without effort the male and female of each species, while the diversity of plumage is calculated to improve the appearance of the whole, and to give to each part its peculiar beauty. The advantage to be drawn from a variety of attitudes is not to be overlooked; and they serve also to indicate something of the particular character of the different birds of which this delightful assemblage is formed.

The third is a *surtout de table* executed in China, according to the ideas of M. Van-Braam: it is composed of seventeen detached pieces.

The middle one, thirty-six inches high, with a base of eight sides (*pans*) twenty-eight inches long by twenty-two broad, is made in the Chinese fashion: that is to say, it represents rocks intersperfed with pagodas, human figures, bridges, trees, fruit, flowers, quadrupeds, birds, insects, &c. The greater part of these things are of silver wrought in different coloured filligree, while the fruit and flowers are of coral, amber, and other substances equally valuable, and even of precious stones. To this assemblage, at once picturesque, noble, and elegant, are added basons and streams of water, in which are fish and crustaceous animals of a variety of kinds, and of the most brilliant and striking appearance.

VOL. II.   Y   The

The two other principal pieces, or *bouts de table*, which are each twenty-six inches high, with an octagonal base twenty-two inches long by eighteen inches broad, correspond in beauty and richness with the middle piece, and are of analogous composition.

All the three display a considerable degree of magnificence resulting from the nature of the objects thus brought together. The eye is attracted by them all, and when after having wandered from part to part, delighted with so much variety, it begins to distinguish the different things employed in these noble compositions, it still hesitates between their different beauties, before the moment comes when its enjoyments are renewed, almost incessantly, by a minute examination of each pagoda, of each figure, of each tree, and of each animal; every one seeming to claim a preference continually disputed by the rest.

Eight other pieces consist of a like number of flower or fruit-bearing trees, surrounded by plants, which add to their effect by harmonies and contrasts equally happy. The coloured gold and silver, the filligram work, the amber, the coral, and precious stones which ornament them, and embellish their different parts, are an additional gratification to the eye. They also contain dishes intended for ragouts and the lighter kinds of viands, which are rendered more inviting by the elegant way in which they are served up.

Finally, six other pieces, serving as so many lustres, round which trees, fruits, flowers, and animals are placed

placed, as if on purpofe, that the light of the candles may exhibit to the greater advantage both their graceful and fingular forms, and the genius with which the Chinefe artift has reprefented every thing, compleat a whole that the *amateur* can never fufficiently admire.

I am fenfible that it is eafy for a perfon who has not feen this *furtout de table*, which is calculated to embellifh the moft diftinguifhed feftival, to think that flattery has directed the pen of him who defcribes it; but any one who has examined it with the attention it deferves, will reproach my pen with having weakened the impreffion it has attempted to re-produce.

The fourth thing I have to fpeak of, is a collection of more than a hundred figures and other articles, all of bamboo, which fhew to what extent fculpture is carried in China, and what degree of perfection a Chinefe hand is capable of arriving at in that delicate fort of work.

Since I have fpoken of two of the pictures of M. Van-Braam, I muft add that in his collection of articles of that kind, there are alfo a great number of copies made by Chinefe painters, either in miniature or oil, and painted on canvafs, glafs, or ivory, from feveral fubjects, originally painted in Europe, and particularly in France. Thefe copies derive from the brilliancy of the colours, and from the ornaments added in China, particularly thofe of the vegetable kingdom, a merit peculiar to themfelves.

In short, the furniture, ornaments, every thing at M. Van-Braam's remind us of China; and the estate he has bought for his own residence at six leagues from Philadelphia, and at a league from Bristol, and which he takes a pleasure in embellishing after the manner of the country he has lately left, will merit, in more than one respect, the name of *The Chinese Retreat*, which he has given it.

THE EDITOR.

[The public will learn with pleasure that M. Van-Braam has offered this valuable collection to the Executive Directory of the French Republic; that the Minister for Foreign Affairs, who is not ignorant of its merit, and who will not be accused of losing any opportunity of favouring artists and the arts, has accepted this handsome offer in the name of the government; and that every one will soon have it in his power to compare the collection with the account given by the editor.]

www.ingramcontent.com/pod-product-compliance
Lightning Source LLC
Chambersburg PA
CBHW030734230426

43667CB00007B/709